Mindset Mathematics

Visualizing and Investigating Big Ideas

Jo Boaler

Jen Munson

Cathy Williams

JB JOSSEY-BASS™

A Wiley Brand

Published by Jossey-Bass
A Wiley Brand
One Montgomery Street, Suite 1000, San Francisco, CA 94104-4594—www.josseybass.com

Jossey-Bass books and products are available through most bookstores. To contact Jossey-Bass directly call our Customer Care Department within the U.S. at 800-956-7739, outside the U.S. at 317-572-3986, or fax 317-572-4002.

Wiley publishes in a variety of print and electronic formats and by print-on-demand. Some material included with standard print versions of this book may not be included in e-books or in print-on-demand. If this book refers to media such as a CD or DVD that is not included in the version you purchased, you may download this material at http://booksupport.wiley.com. For more information about Wiley products, visit www.wiley.com.

The Visualize, Play, and Investigate icons are used under license from Shutterstock.com and the following arists: Blan-k, Marish, and SuzanaM.

Library of Congress Cataloging-in-Publication Data

Names: Boaler, Jo, 1964– author. | Munson, Jen, 1977– author. | Williams, Cathy, 1962– author.
Title: Mindset mathematics : visualizing and investigating big ideas, grade 3 / by Jo Boaler, Jen Munson, Cathy Williams.
Description: San Francisco, CA : Jossey-Bass, [2018] | Includes index.
Identifiers: LCCN 2018015426 (print) | LCCN 2018017774 (ebook) | ISBN 9781119358657 (pdf) | ISBN 9781119358794 (epub) | ISBN 9781119358701 (pbk.)
Subjects: LCSH: Games in mathematics education. | Mathematics–Study and teaching (Elementary)–Activity programs. | Third grade (Education)
Classification: LCC QA20.G35 (ebook) | LCC QA20.G35 B6295 2018 (print) | DDC 372.7/043–dc23
LC record available at https://lccn.loc.gov/2018015426

Cover design by Wiley
Cover image: © Marish/Shutterstock-Eye; © Kritchanut/iStockphoto-Background
Printed in the United States of America

FIRST EDITION

V10008509_030119

Contents

To all those teachers pursuing a mathematical mindset journey with us.

Introduction

I still remember the moment when Youcubed, the Stanford center I direct, was conceived. I was at the Denver NCSM and NCTM conferences in 2013, and I had arranged to meet Cathy Williams, the director of mathematics for Vista Unified School District. Cathy and I had been working together for the past year improving mathematics teaching in her district. We had witnessed amazing changes taking place, and a filmmaker had documented some of the work. I had recently released my online teacher course, called How to Learn Math, and been overwhelmed by requests from tens of thousands of teachers to provide them with more of the same ideas. Cathy and I decided to create a website and use it to continue sharing the ideas we had used in her district and that I had shared in my online class. Soon after we started sharing ideas on the Youcubed website, we were invited to become a Stanford University center, and Cathy became the codirector of the center with me.

In the months that followed, with the help of one of my undergraduates, Montse Cordero, our first version of youcubed.org was launched. By January 2015, we had managed to raise some money and hire engineers, and we launched a revised version of the site that is close to the site you may know today. We were very excited that in the first month of that relaunch, we had five thousand visits to the site. At the time of writing this, we are now getting three million visits to the site each month. Teachers are excited to learn about the new research and to take the tools, videos, and activities that translate research ideas into practice and use them in their teaching.

Low-Floor, High-Ceiling Tasks

One of the most popular articles on our website is called "Fluency without Fear." I wrote this with Cathy when I heard from many teachers that they were being made to use timed tests in the elementary grades. At the same time, new brain science was emerging showing that when people feel stressed—as students do when facing a timed test—part of their brain, the working memory, is restricted. The working memory is exactly the area of the brain that comes into play when students need to calculate with math facts, and this is the exact area that is impeded when students are stressed. We have evidence now that suggests strongly that timed math tests in the early grades are responsible for the early onset of math anxiety for many students. I teach an undergraduate class at Stanford, and many of the undergraduates are math traumatized. When I ask them what happened to cause this, almost all of them will recall, with startling clarity, the time in elementary school when they were given timed tests. We are really pleased that "Fluency without Fear" has now been used across the United States to pull timed tests out of school districts. It has been downloaded many thousands of times and used in state and national hearings.

One of the reasons for the amazing success of the paper is that it does not just share the brain science on the damage of timed tests but also offers an alternative to timed tests: activities that teach math facts conceptually and through activities that students and teachers enjoy. One of the activities—a game called How Close to 100—became so popular that thousands of teachers tweeted photos of their students playing the game. There was so much attention on Twitter and other media that Stanford noticed and decided to write a news story on the damage of speed to mathematics learning. This was picked up by news outlets across the United States, including *US News & World Report*, which is part of the reason the white paper has now had so many downloads and so much impact. Teachers themselves caused this mini revolution by spreading news of the activities and research.

How Close to 100 is just one of many tasks we have on youcubed.org that are extremely popular with teachers and students. All our tasks have the feature of being "low floor and high ceiling," which I consider to be an extremely important quality for engaging all students in a class. If you are teaching only one student, then a mathematics task can be fairly narrow in terms of its content and difficulty. But whenever you have a group of students, there will be differences in their needs, and they will be challenged by different ideas. A low-floor, high-ceiling task is one in which everyone can engage, no matter what his or her prior understanding or knowledge, but also one that is open enough to extend to high levels so that all students can be deeply challenged. In the last two years, we have launched an introductory week of mathematics lessons on our site that are open, visual, and low floor, high ceiling. These have been extremely popular with teachers; they have had approximately four million downloads and are used in 20% of schools across the United States.

In our extensive work with teachers around the United States, we are continually asked for more tasks that are like those on our website. Most textbook publishers seem to ignore or be unaware of research on mathematics learning, and most textbook questions are narrow and insufficiently engaging for students. It is imperative that the new knowledge of the ways our brains learn mathematics is incorporated into the lessons students are given in classrooms. It is for this reason that we chose to write a series of books that are organized around a principle of active student engagement, that reflect the latest brain science on learning, and that include activities that are low floor and high ceiling.

Youcubed Summer Camp

We recently brought 81 students onto the Stanford campus for a Youcubed summer math camp, to teach them in the ways that are encouraged in this book. We used open, creative, and visual math tasks. After only 18 lessons with us, the students improved their test score performance by an average of 50%, the equivalent of 1.6 years of school. More important, they changed their relationship with mathematics and started believing in their own potential. They did this, in part, because we talked to them about the brain science showing that

- There is no such thing as a math person—anyone can learn mathematics to high levels.
- Mistakes, struggle, and challenge are critical for brain growth.
- Speed is unimportant in mathematics.
- Mathematics is a visual and beautiful subject, and our brains want to think visually about mathematics.

All of these messages were key to the students' changed mathematics relationship, but just as critical were the tasks we worked on in class. The tasks and the messages about the brain were perfect complements to each other, as we told students they could learn anything, and we showed them a mathematics that was open, creative, and engaging. This approach helped them see that they could learn mathematics and actually do so. This book shares the kinds of tasks that we used in our summer camp, that make up our week of inspirational mathematics (WIM) lessons, and that we post on our site.

Before I outline and introduce the different sections of the book and the ways we are choosing to engage students, I will share some important ideas about how students learn mathematics.

Memorization versus Conceptual Engagement

Many students get the wrong idea about mathematics—exactly the wrong idea. Through years of mathematics classes, many students come to believe that their role in mathematics learning is to memorize methods and facts, and that mathematics success comes from memorization. I say this is exactly the wrong idea because there is actually very little to remember in mathematics. The subject is made up of a few big, linked ideas, and students who are successful in mathematics are those who see the subject as a set of ideas that they need to think deeply about. The Program for International Student Assessment (PISA) tests are international assessments of mathematics, reading, and science that are given every three years. In 2012, PISA not only assessed mathematics achievement but also collected data on students' approach to mathematics. I worked with the PISA team in Paris at the Organisation for Economic Co-operation and Development (OECD) to analyze students' mathematics approaches and their relationship to achievement. One clear result emerged from this analysis. Students approached mathematics in three distinct ways. One group approached mathematics by attempting to memorize the methods they had met; another group took a "relational" approach, relating new concepts to those they already knew; and a third group took a self-monitoring approach, thinking about what they knew and needed to know.

In every country, the memorizers were the lowest-achieving students, and countries with high numbers of memorizers were all lower achieving. In no country were memorizers in the highest-achieving group, and in some high-achieving countries such as Japan, students who combined self-monitoring and relational strategies outscored memorizing students by more than a year's worth of schooling. More detail on this finding is given in this *Scientific American* Mind article that I coauthored with a PISA analyst: https://www.scientificamerican.com/article/why-math-education-in-the-u-s-doesn-t-add-up/.

Mathematics is a conceptual subject, and it is important for students to be thinking slowly, deeply, and conceptually about mathematical ideas, not racing through methods that they try to memorize. One reason that students need to think conceptually has to do with the ways the brain processes mathematics. When we learn new mathematical ideas, they take up a large space in our brain as the brain works out where they fit and what they connect with. But with time, as we move on with our understanding, the knowledge becomes compressed in the brain, taking up a very small space. For first graders, the idea of addition takes up a large space in their brains as they think about how it works and what it means, but for adults the idea of addition is compressed, and it takes up a small space. When adults are asked to add 2 and 3, for example, they can quickly and easily extract the compressed knowledge. William Thurston (1990), a mathematician who won the Field's Medal—the highest honor in mathematics—explains compression like this:

> Mathematics is amazingly compressible: you may struggle a long time, step by step, to work through the same process or idea from several approaches. But once you really understand it and have the mental perspective to see it as a whole, there is often a tremendous mental compression. You can file it away, recall it quickly and completely when you need it, and use it as just one step in some other mental process. The insight that goes with this compression is one of the real joys of mathematics.

You will probably agree with me that not many students think of mathematics as a "real joy," and part of the reason is that they are not compressing mathematical ideas in their brain. This is because the brain only compresses concepts, not methods. So if students are thinking that mathematics is a set of methods to memorize, they are on the wrong pathway, and it is critical that we change that. It is very important that students think deeply and conceptually about ideas. We provide the activities in this book that will allow students to think deeply and conceptually, and an essential role of the teacher is to give the students time to do so.

Mathematical Thinking, Reasoning, and Convincing

When we worked with our Youcubed camp students, we gave each of them journals to record their mathematical thinking. I am a big fan of journaling—for myself and my students. For mathematics students, it helps show them that mathematics is a subject for which we should record ideas and pictures. We can use journaling to encourage students to keep organized records, which is another important part of mathematics, and help them understand that mathematical thinking can be a long and slow process. Journals also give students free space—where they can be creative, share ideas, and feel ownership of their work. We did not write in the students' journals, as we wanted them to think of the journals as their space, not something that teachers wrote on. We gave students feedback on sticky notes that we stuck onto their work. The images in Figure I.1 show some of the mathematical records the camp students kept in their journals.

Another resource I always share with learners is the act of color coding—that is, students using colors to highlight different ideas. For example, when working on an algebraic task, they may show the x in the same color in an expression, in a graph, and in a picture, as shown in Figure I.2. When adding numbers, color coding may help show the addends (Figure I.3).

Color coding highlights connections, which are a really critical part of mathematics.

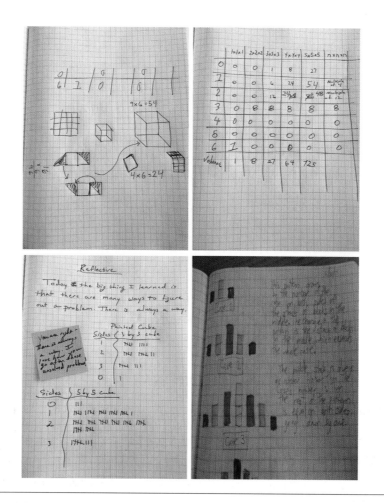

Figure I.1

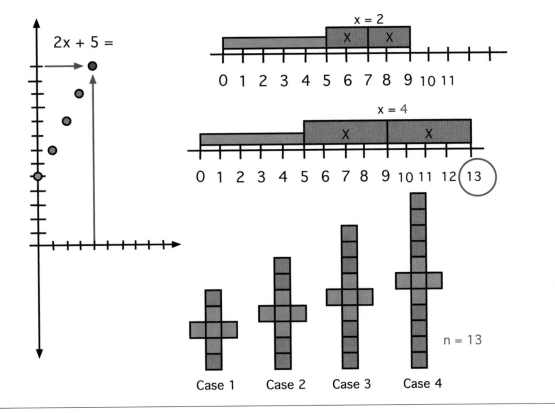

Figure I.2

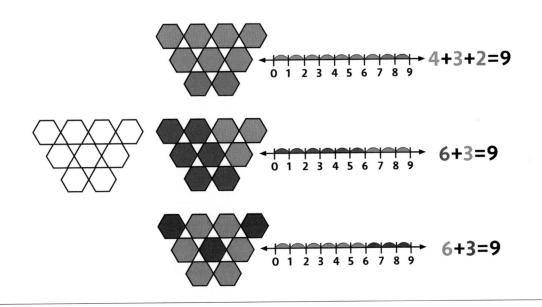

Figure I.3

Another important part of mathematics is the act of reasoning—explaining why methods are chosen and how steps are linked, and using logic to connect ideas. Reasoning is at the heart of mathematics. Scientists prove ideas by finding more cases that fit a theory, or countercases that contradict a theory, but mathematicians prove their work by reasoning. If students are not reasoning, then they are not really doing mathematics. In the activities of these books, we suggest a framework that encourages students to be convincing when they reason. We tell them that there are three levels of being convincing. The first, or easiest, level is to convince yourself of something. A higher level is to convince a friend. And the highest level of all is to convince a skeptic. We also share with students that they should be skeptics with one another, asking one another why methods were chosen and how they work. We have found this framework to be very powerful with students; they enjoy being skeptics, pushing each other to deeper levels of reasoning, and it encourages students to reason clearly, which is important for their learning.

We start each book in our series with an activity that invites students to reason about mathematics and be convincing. I first met an activity like this when reading Mark Driscoll's teaching ideas in his book *Fostering Algebraic Thinking*. I thought it was a perfect activity for introducing the skeptics framework that I had learned from a wonderful teacher, Cathy Humphreys. She had learned about and adapted the framework from two of my inspirational teachers from England: mathematician John Mason and mathematics educator Leone Burton. As well as encouraging students to be convincing, in a number of activities we ask students to prove an idea. Some people think of proof as a formal set of steps that they learned in geometry class. But the act of proving is really about connecting ideas, and as students enter the learning journey of proving, it is worthwhile celebrating their steps toward formal proof. Mathematician Paul Lockhart (2012) rejects the idea that proving is about following a set of formal steps, instead proposing that proving is "abstract art, pure and simple. And art is always a struggle. There is no systematic way of creating beautiful and meaningful paintings or sculptures, and there is also no method for producing beautiful and meaningful mathematical arguments" (p. 8). Instead of suggesting that students follow formal steps, we invite them to think deeply about mathematical concepts and make connections. Students will be given many ways to be creative when they prove and justify, and for reasons I discuss later, we always encourage and celebrate visual as well as numerical and algebraic justifications. Ideally, students will create visual, numerical, and algebraic representations and connect their ideas through color coding and through verbal explanations. Students are excited to experience mathematics in these ways, and they benefit from the opportunity to bring their individual ideas and creativity to the problem-solving and learning space. As students develop in their mathematical understanding, we can encourage them to extend and generalize their ideas through reasoning, justifying, and proving. This process deepens their understanding and helps them compress their learning.

Big Ideas

The books in the Mindset Mathematics Series are all organized around mathematical "big ideas." Mathematics is not a set of methods; it is a set of connected ideas that need to be understood. When students understand the big ideas in mathematics, the methods and rules fall into place. One of the reasons any set of curriculum standards is flawed is that standards take the beautiful subject of mathematics and its many connections, and divide it into small pieces that make the connections disappear. Instead of starting with the small pieces, we have started with the big ideas and important connections, and have listed the relevant Common Core curriculum standards within the activities. Our activities invite students to engage in the mathematical acts that are listed in the imperative Common Core practice standards, and they also teach many of the Common Core content standards, which emerge from the rich activities. Student activity pages are noted with a and teacher activity pages are noted with a 🖥.

Although we have chapters for each big idea, as though they are separate from each other, they are all intrinsically linked. Figure I.4 shows some of the connections between the ideas, and you may be able to see others. It is very important to share with students that mathematics is a subject of connections and to highlight the connections as students work. You may want to print the color visual of the different connections for students to see as they work. To see the maps of big ideas for all of the grades K through 8, find our paper "What Is Mathematical Beauty?" at youcubed.org.

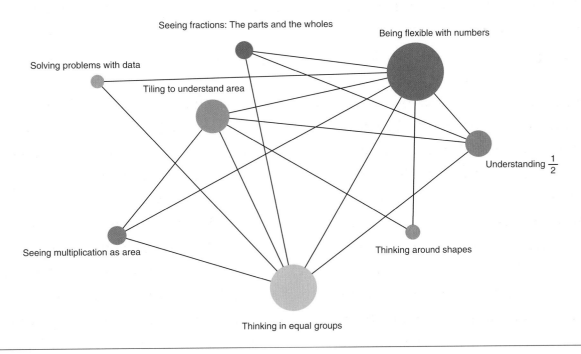

Figure I.4

Structure of the Book

Visualize. Play. Investigate. These three words provide the structure for each book in the series. They also pave the way for open student thinking, for powerful brain connections, for engagement, and for deep understanding. How do they do that? And why is this book so different from other mathematics curriculum books?

Visualize

For the past few years, I have been working with a neuroscience group at Stanford, under the direction of Vinod Menon, which specializes in mathematics learning. We have been working together to think about the ways that findings from brain science can be used to help learners of mathematics. One of the exciting discoveries that has been emerging over the last few years is the importance of visualizing for the brain and our learning of mathematics. Brain scientists now know that when we work on mathematics, even when we perform a bare number calculation, five areas of the brain are involved, as shown in Figure I.5.

Two of the five brain pathways—the dorsal and ventral pathways—are visual. The dorsal visual pathway is the main brain region for representing quantity. This may seem

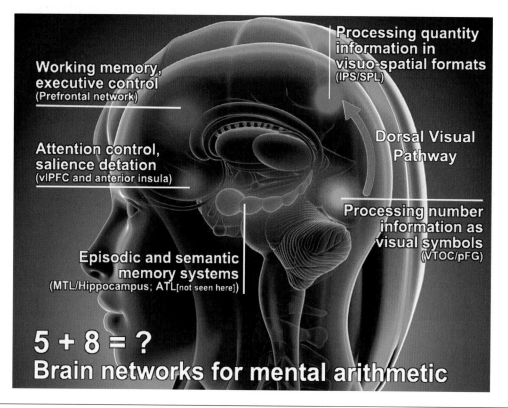

Figure I.5

surprising, as so many of us have sat through hundreds of hours of mathematics classes working with numbers, while barely ever engaging visually with mathematics. Now brain scientists know that our brains "see" fingers when we calculate, and knowing fingers well—what they call finger perception—is critical for the development of an understanding of number. If you would like to read more about the importance of finger work in mathematics, look at the visual mathematics section of youcubed.org. Number lines are really helpful, as they provide the brain with a visual representation of number order. In one study, a mere four 15-minute sessions of students playing with a number line completely eradicated the differences between students from low-income and middle-income backgrounds coming into school (Siegler & Ramani, 2008).

Our brain wants to think visually about mathematics, yet few curriculum materials engage students in visual thinking. Some mathematics books show pictures, but they rarely ever invite students to do their own visualizing and drawing. The neuroscientists' research shows the importance not only of visual thinking but also of students' connecting different areas of their brains as they work on mathematics. The scientists now know that as children learn and develop, they increase the connections between different parts of the brain, and they particularly develop connections between symbolic and visual representations of numbers. Increased mathematics achievement comes about when students are developing those connections. For so long, our emphasis in mathematics education has been on symbolic representations of numbers, with students developing one area of the brain that is concerned with symbolic number representation. A more productive and engaging approach is to develop all areas of the brain that are involved in mathematical thinking, and visual connections are critical to this development.

In addition to the brain development that occurs when students think visually, we have found that visual activities are really engaging for students. Even students who think they are "not visual learners" (an incorrect idea) become fascinated and think deeply about mathematics that is shown visually—such as the visual representations of the calculation 18 × 5 shown in Figure I.6.

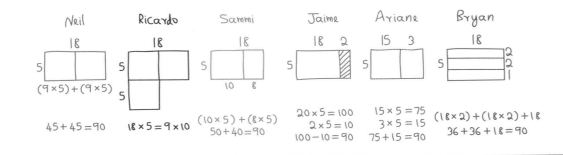

Figure I.6

In our Youcubed teaching of summer school to sixth- and seventh-grade students and in our trialing of Youcubed's WIM materials, we have found that students are inspired by the creativity that is possible when mathematics is visual. When we were trialing the materials in a local middle school one day, a parent stopped me and asked what we had been doing. She said that her daughter had always said she hated and couldn't do math, but after working on our tasks, she came home saying she could see a future for herself in mathematics. We had been working on the number visuals that we use throughout these teaching materials, shown in Figure I.7.

The parent reported that when her daughter had seen the creativity possible in mathematics, everything had changed for her. I strongly believe that we can give these insights and inspirations to many more learners with the sort of creative, open mathematics tasks that fill this book.

We have also found that when we present visual activities to students, the status differences that often get in the way of good mathematics teaching disappear. I was visiting a first-grade classroom recently, and the teacher had set up four different stations around the room. In all of them, the students were working on arithmetic. In one, the teacher engaged students in a mini number talk; in another, a teaching

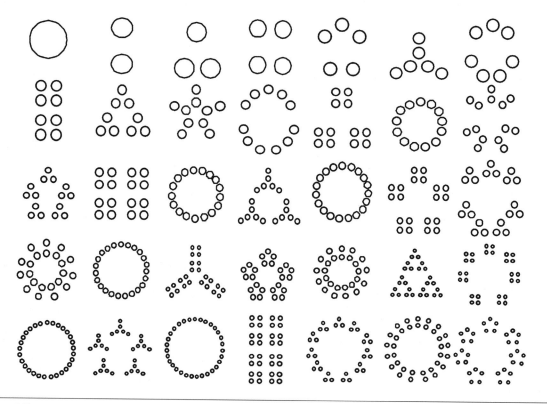

Figure I.7

assistant worked on an activity with coins; in the third, the students played a board game; and in the fourth, they worked on a number worksheet. In each of the first three stations, the students collaborated and worked really well, but as soon as students went to the worksheet station, conversations changed, and in every group I heard statements like "This is easy," " I've finished," "I can't do this," and "Haven't you finished yet?" These status comments are unfortunate and off-putting for many students. I now try to present mathematical tasks without numbers as often as possible, or I take out the calculation part of a task, as it is the numerical and calculational aspects that often cause students to feel less sure of themselves. This doesn't mean that students cannot have a wonderful and productive relationship with numbers, as we hope to promote in this book, but sometimes the key mathematical idea can be arrived at without any numbers at all.

Almost all the tasks in our book invite students to think visually about mathematics and to connect visual and numerical representations. This encourages important brain connections as well as deep student engagement.

Play

The key to reducing status differences in mathematics classrooms, in my view, comes from *opening* mathematics. When we teach students that we can see or approach any mathematical idea in different ways, they start to respect the different thinking of all students. Opening mathematics involves inviting students to see ideas differently, explore with ideas, and ask their own questions. Students can gain access to the same mathematical ideas and methods through creativity and exploration that they can by being taught methods that they practice. As well as reducing or removing status differences, open mathematics is more engaging for students. This is why we are inviting students, through these mathematics materials, to play with mathematics. Albert Einstein famously once said that "play is the highest form of research." This is because play is an opportunity for ideas to be used and developed in the service of something enjoyable. In the Play activities of our materials, students are invited to work with an important idea in a free space where they can enjoy the freedom of mathematical play. This does not mean that the activities do not teach essential mathematical content and practices—they do, as they invite students to work with the ideas. We have designed the Play activities to downplay competition and instead invite students to work with each other, building understanding together.

Investigate ❓

Our Investigate activities add something very important: they give students opportunities to take ideas to the sky. They also have a playful element, but the difference is that they pose questions that students can explore and take to very high levels. As I mentioned earlier, all of our tasks are designed to be as low floor and high ceiling as possible, as these provide the best conditions for engaging all students, whatever their prior knowledge. Any student can access them, and students can take the ideas to high levels. We should always be open to being surprised by what our learners can do, and always provide all students with opportunities to take work to high levels and to be challenged.

A crucial finding from neuroscience is the importance of students struggling and making mistakes—these are the times when brains grow the most. In one of my meetings with a leading neuroscientist, he stated it very clearly: if students are not struggling, they are not learning. We want to put students into situations where they feel that work is hard, but within their reach. Do not worry if students ask questions that you don't know the answer to; that is a good thing. One of the damaging ideas that teachers and students share in education is that teachers of mathematics know everything. This gives students the idea that mathematics people are those who know a lot and never make mistakes, which is an incorrect and harmful message. It is good to say to your students, "That is a great question that we can all think about" or "I have never thought about that idea; let's investigate it together." It is even good to make mistakes in front of students, as it shows them that mistakes are an important part of mathematical work. As they investigate, they should be going to places you have never thought about—taking ideas in new directions and exploring uncharted territory. Model for students what it means to be a curious mathematics learner, always open to learning new ideas and being challenged yourself.

* * *

We have designed activities to take at least a class period, but some of them could go longer, especially if students ask deep questions or start an investigation into a cool idea. If you can be flexible about students' time on activities, that is ideal, or you may wish to suggest that students continue activities at home. In our teaching of these activities, we have found that students are so excited by the ideas that they take them home to their families and continue working on them, which is wonderful. At all times, celebrate deep thinking over speed, as that is the nature of real mathematical thought. Ask students to come up with creative representations of their ideas; celebrate their drawing, modeling, and any form of creativity. Invite your students into a journey of mathematical curiosity and take that journey with them, walking by their side as they experience the wonder of open, mindset mathematics.

References

Lockhart, P. (2012). *Measurement.* Cambridge, MA: Harvard University Press.

Siegler, R. S., & Ramani, G. B. (2008). Playing linear numerical board games promotes low income children's numerical development. *Developmental Science, 11*(5), 655–661. doi:10.1111/j.1467-7687.2008.00714.x

Thurston, W. (1990). Mathematical education. *Notices of the American Mathematical Society, 37*(7), 844–850.

Activities for Building Norms

Encouraging Good Group Work

We always use this activity before students work on math together, as it helps improve group interactions. Teachers who have tried this activity have been pleased by students' thoughtful responses and found the students' thoughts and words helpful in creating a positive and supportive environment. The first thing to do is to ask students, in groups, to reflect on things they don't like people to say or do in a group when they are working on math together. Students come up with quite a few important ideas, such as not liking people to give away the answer, to rush through the work, or to ignore other people's ideas. When students have had enough time in groups brainstorming, collect the ideas. We usually do this by making a What We Don't Like list or poster and asking each group to contribute one idea, moving around the room until a few good ideas have been shared (usually about 10). Then we do the same for the What We Do Like list or poster. It can be good to present the final posters to the class as the agreed-on classroom norms that you and they can reflect back on over the year. If any student shares a negative comment, such as "I don't like waiting for slow people," do not put it on the poster; instead use it as a chance to discuss the issue. This rarely happens, and students are usually very thoughtful and respectful in the ideas they share.

Activity	Time	Description/Prompt	Materials
Launch	5 min	Explain to students that working in groups is an important part of what mathematicians do. Mathematicians discuss their ideas and work together to solve challenging problems. It's important to work together, and we need to discuss what helps us work well together.	
Explore	10 min	Assign a group facilitator to make sure that all students get to share their thoughts on points 1 and 2. Groups should record every group member's ideas and then decide which they will share during the whole-class discussion. In your groups . . . 1. Reflect on the things you do not like people to say or do when you are working on math together in a group. 2. Reflect on the things you do like people to say or do when you are working on math together in a group.	• Paper • Pencil or pen
Discuss	10 min	Ask each group to share their findings. Condense their responses and make a poster so that the student ideas are visible and you can refer to them during the class.	Two to four pieces of large poster paper to collect the students' ideas

Paper Folding: Learning to Reason, Convince, and Be Skeptical

> **Connection to CCSS**
> 3.G.3
> 3.G.4

One of the most important topics in mathematics is reasoning. Whereas scientists prove or disprove ideas by finding cases, mathematicians prove their ideas by reasoning—making logical connections between ideas. This activity gives students an opportunity to learn to reason well by having to convince others who are being skeptical.

Before beginning the activity, explain to students that their role is to be convincing. The easiest person to convince is yourself. A higher level of being convincing is to convince a friend, and the highest level of all is to convince a skeptic. In this activity, the students learn to reason to the extent that they can convince a skeptic. Students should work in pairs and take turns to be the one convincing and the one being a skeptic.

Give each student a square piece of paper. If you already have 8.5 × 11 paper, you can ask them to make the square first.

The first challenge is for one of the students to fold the paper to make a rectangle that does not include any of the edges of the paper. They should convince their partner that it is a rectangle, using what she knows about rectangles to be convincing. The skeptic partner should ask lots of skeptical questions, such as "How do you know that the angles are all right angles?" and not accept that they are because it looks like they are.

The partners should then switch roles, and the other student folds the paper into a square that does not include any of the edges of the paper. Their partner should be skeptical and push for high levels of reasoning.

The partners should then switch again, and the challenge is to fold the paper to make a triangle, again not using the edges of the paper.

The fourth challenge is to make a different triangle. For each challenge, partners must reason and be skeptical.

When the task is complete, facilitate a whole-class discussion in which students discuss the following questions:

- Which was the most challenging task? Why?
- What was hard about reasoning and being convincing?
- What was hard about being a skeptic?

Activity	Time	Description/Prompt	Materials
Launch	5 min	Tell students that their role for the day is to be convincing and to be a skeptic. Ask students to fold a piece of paper into a rectangle that is not a square. Choose a student and model being a skeptic.	
Explore	10 min	Show students the task and explain that in each round, they are to solve the folding problem. In pairs, students alternate folding and reasoning and being the skeptic. After students convince themselves they have solved each problem, they switch roles and fold the next challenge. Give students square paper or ask them to start by making a square. The convincing challenges are as follows: 1. Fold your paper into a rectangle that does not include any edges of the paper. 2. Fold your paper into a square that does not include any edges of the paper. 3. Fold your paper into a triangle that does not include any edges of the paper. 4. Fold your paper into a different triangle that does not include any edges of the paper.	• One piece of 8.5" × 11" paper per student • Paper Folding worksheet for each student
Discuss	10 min	Discuss the activity as a class. Make sure to discuss the roles of convincer and skeptic.	

Paper Folding: Learning to Reason, Convince, and Be a Skeptic

1. Fold your paper into a rectangle that does not include any edges of the paper. Convince a skeptic that it is a rectangle.
   Reflection:

   Switch roles

2. Fold your paper into a square that does not include any edges of the paper. Convince a skeptic that it is a square.
   Reflection:

   Switch roles

3. Fold your paper into a triangle that does not include any edges of the paper. Convince a skeptic that it is a triangle.
   Reflection:

   Switch roles

4. Fold your paper into a different triangle that does not include any edges of the paper. Convince a skeptic that it is a triangle.
   Reflection:

BIG IDEA 1

Solving Problems with Data

We begin this grade 3 book with a topic that is extremely important to the 21st century but that is often left out because of time constraints. Textbook publishers often place measurement and data at the end of books, but we have chosen to open with this topic to acknowledge its importance. The activities in this big idea give students opportunities to explore and understand their world—inviting them to ask their own questions and discuss the relevance of data. There can be few more critical activities in which students engage as they learn to be mathematically literate citizens.

In the Visualize activity, we invite students to wonder about the lengths of animal tongues, which should be interesting and engaging. Students are also asked to read a bar graph and work to interpret what it is telling them. We have chosen some animals we think students may be curious about. We encourage you to allow students time to investigate and find out more about the animals. As students work to make sense of graphs and data, they will develop quantitative literacy, which is an extremely important attribute. As students read the graph and work to understand what it is telling them, they will need to pay careful attention to the way the vertical axis is numbered. Later in the activity, we provide students with tables of data and ask them to create visual images that communicate the data. This lesson is inspired by a book by Steve Jenkins, *Animals by the Numbers.* Having this book available for students would be a nice addition to the lesson.

The Play activity provides students an opportunity to use what they learned in the previous lesson as they inspect a graph that has some mistakes. One of the most debilitating ideas for learners is the myth that they always have to be right.

Our Youcubed team has worked hard to dispel this myth by communicating the neuroscience which shows that when students are struggling and making mistakes, brain growth occurs. This lesson is a good time to celebrate the value of mistakes and communicate the brain science information that we also share here: https://www.youcubed.org/resource/brain-science/. Students in this lesson are again encouraged to develop quantitative literacy by reading graphs that display data, and noticing and discussing the mistakes in the graph. It is important to embrace the mistakes and talk about mistakes in playful rather than pejorative tones. Students then get the opportunity to make their own mischievous graph where they can try to mislead their peers with a display that contains mistakes. We think students will love playing Inspector Graph-It.

In the Investigate activity, students investigate a real question about the most common car color in their area. They will pose the question and determine together a data collection plan. Later they will take the data and interpret it to answer the question about car color. This provides an opportunity for students to think about a real question and also consider together why this could be useful information. The extension in this activity is worth the extra days. Students have an opportunity to ask their own questions and collect data. An important goal for us as mathematics educators is to give students opportunities to act with agency—to use their own thoughts and ideas as they work mathematically. It is very helpful to give students opportunities to ask their own questions—instead of only answering questions that have been given to them. When students ask their own questions of data, we achieve both of these goals.

Jo Boaler

Tongues, Tails, and in Between

Snapshot

Students investigate a graph of the lengths of different animals' tongues to develop ways of interpreting data displays, with a focus on reading a scaled axis. Then students choose a set of animal measurement data and create their own data displays to compare and discuss.

Connection to CCSS
3.MD.3
3.NBT.2, 3.NF.1, 3.OA.3

Agenda

Activity	Time	Description/Prompt	Materials
Launch	5–10 min	Show students the Animal Tongue Lengths graph on a projector and ask what the graph shows. Collect students' observations and the reasoning behind them.	Animal Tongue Lengths graph, to display
Explore	20–25 min	Partners record their observations of the data in the Animal Tongue Lengths graph. Using these interpretations, partners may construct alternative data displays.	• Copies of the Animal Tongue Lengths graph, one per partnership • Optional: 1" grid paper (see appendix)
Discuss	10–15 min	Discuss the observations students made of the Animal Tongue Lengths graph and how they read the measurements on the scaled vertical axis. Discuss students' alternative data displays, for those who made them, and compare the ways the data is shown.	Animal Tongue Lengths graph, to display

(Continued)

Activity	Time	Description/Prompt	Materials
Explore	20–30 min	Partners choose one of four Animal Data Tables and make observations about the data. Partners then create a data display that communicates what they think is most interesting in the data.	• Animal Data Tables, copied and cut into quarters to provide choices for partners • Make available: 1" grid paper (see appendix), colors
Discuss	15+ min	Students do a gallery walk of the data displays others have created and leave sticky notes with observations and questions. The class discusses what different displays communicate and what makes a data display interesting.	Small sticky notes

To the Teacher

In this lesson, which can extend across two days, students begin to think about how data can be visual, and the relationship between data and displays. As adults we often have a great deal of comfort with the kinds of data displays used in third grade, and understanding these images comes quickly. But for children, these images don't immediately make data obvious; it takes experience interpreting data displays to become fluent in this visual form of reading. This lesson is designed to give students the opportunity to read displays without the need to answer particular questions imposed from the outside. Instead, we hope to inspire wonder. The bar graph we've constructed to launch this lesson, based on the beautiful data in Steve Jenkins's book *Animals by the Numbers,* is intended to be intriguing and to get students wondering about the data and the unusual animals it represents. If students want to find pictures of these animals or investigate in other ways, we encourage you to support their curiosity. If you have access to *Animals by the Numbers,* we encourage you to make this book available to students to explore the many creative ways Jenkins displays and communicates data.

The graph poses a mathematical challenge important for students to grapple with. The vertical axis is scaled in increments of 5, rather than one, and not all of the data falls neatly into multiples of 5. Students need to attend to these increments to measure the length of a bar, and they will need to think proportionately to estimate how long a tongue might be that falls between two increments. Encourage students to make their thinking about these estimates public and discuss which inferences are reasonable and which are not convincing. Several mathematical concepts intersect when students are doing this work, and it is useful to bear in mind all that students are working to integrate. Students need to think in terms of equal groups and skip counting to interpret (and construct) the scaled axis; they need to be thinking about differences on a scale to interpret comparisons; they need to interpret the axis as a number line and think fractionally about the values between increments. Any one of these concepts could provide productive struggle for students as they work first to interpret and then to construct graphs.

Activity

Launch

Launch this lesson by showing students the Animal Tongue Lengths graph on a projector. Ask students what they notice in the graph, or, What does this image show? Give students a few moments to turn and talk to a partner about the graph. Collect from students a few of their observations about the graph. Encourage students to come up to the graph to point out the specific features or data points they notice. Press students to explain any inferences they have made. For instance, students might infer that one animal's tongue is longer than another. You'll want to ask students to point out the specific feature of the graph that communicates that idea. Students might connect a bar with an animal's name or with a measure on the vertical axis. Be sure to probe how they made this connection. Use this brief discussion to encourage students to notice details and make their reasoning public before sending them off to make observations with a partner. Tell students that today they will be exploring this graph and trying to figure out all it is telling us.

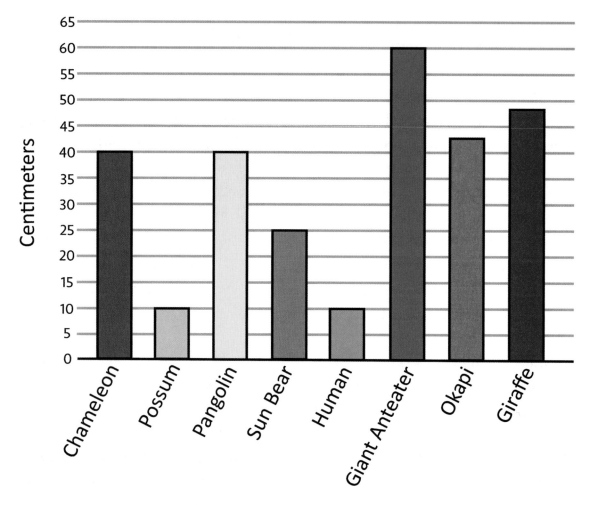

Animal Tongue Lengths

Explore

Students work in partners to make observations about the Animal Tongue Lengths graph. Provide each partnership with a copy of the graph. Students record their observations directly on the graph as annotations. Students can use words, numbers, arrows, or other ways to indicate what they are noticing about what the graph communicates. Encourage students also to pose their own questions of the graph and record these as well.

If students collect many observations about the data, you might challenge them to come up with another way to show this same information. They might create a table, list, or another graph. Encourage students to experiment with ways to show the data. Students' attempts will likely be incomplete or unconventional, but this activity will engage students in trying to capture data in different ways. Make grid paper available (see appendix) for those who'd like.

Discuss

Gather students together and ask them to contribute their observations of the graph. Annotate a shared class graph on the projector with what students noticed.

- Ask, What do you notice? How did the graph communicate that information?
- If students notice comparisons, such as one animal's tongue is longer than another's, ask, How much longer? How do we know? Note that these differences may be estimates, and their reasoning should convince the class, even if multiple estimates are reasonable.

Be sure to draw attention to how to read the measurements when students are making claims about the data shown. Ask students how they read the scale on the side for any measurements they interpret.

If students made alternative data displays, invite them to share what they created and how they thought about communicating the data. Ask the class to make connections between different displays. For instance, you might point out a particular data point and ask the class how the different displays show that information. Ask the class how the different displays help them see the data, or how different displays make it harder to see the data.

Explore

Provide students with the choice of four data tables: Tail Length, Tooth Length, Brain Weight, and Horn Length. Show the data tables on the screen to introduce students to their choices. Invite partners to choose a data set to work with. Provide copies of 1" grid paper (see appendix) and colors.

Partners first need to look at the data and decide what's interesting. Ask student to explore, What does the data show? Then partners create a graph to show the data in their chosen set. Encourage students to organize the data to help others notice what's interesting about their data. They might choose to display all or only part of the data in the table. Students may choose to construct a bar graph similar to the Animal Tongue Lengths graph, or a different data display, such as a pictograph. The key is that students are selecting ways to show what they want others to notice about their data. Be sure students give their data display a title and other labels to help the reader interpret the data shown.

For an optional extension, you may want to invite students to add new data to their tables and displays. If you have resources in your classroom, on the Internet, or in the school library, students could add another animal or two to their data that they think offers an interesting comparison with the existing data.

Discuss

Ask partners to post their data displays around the classroom, either by putting them on the walls or by laying them out on their tables. Do a gallery walk, in which partners walk around looking at the different graphs created. As students look, ask them to consider the following questions:

- What do you learn from the graph?
- What questions does it raise?

Provide students with small sticky notes on which to record their observations and questions. After students have had the chance to look at the different displays, gather the class to discuss the following questions:

- What did you learn from the different graphs? How did the graphs help you learn that?
- What made the different graphs interesting, helpful, or informative?
- What did you notice looking at different graphs of the same data? How did people organize the data differently to show different things?

Invite partners to look at the sticky notes people left for them. Ask partners to discuss with one another, What did others learn or ask? What would you do differently next time? As a whole class, discuss the following reflection questions:

- Did others notice what you hoped they would in your data?
- What did others notice in your data that surprised you?
- What would you revise in your data display to make it more interesting or to better show the data? Why?

Look-Fors

- **How are students interpreting the scale of the graph?** Be sure to support students in attending to the numerical labels on the vertical axis and noticing that they count by 5s. Students may struggle with understanding the meaning of the space between two multiples of 5. It may help students to first focus on an animal with a tongue length that is a multiple of 5, and ask them how long the tongue is. Ask students what the horizontal lines are for or how they help us. Ask, What does it mean when a bar is a little above or a little below a line? What does it mean when a bar is right between two lines?

- **Are students being precise about comparisons?** Students may make qualitative comparisons between tongue lengths, simply saying that one is longer or shorter, or way longer or much shorter, than another. Encourage students to name precisely how much longer or shorter using the graph. To make precise comparisons, students will need either to interpret the two lengths and subtract them or to focus on the vertical distance between the two bars and reason about that difference. To help students think about differences, you might draw students' attention to two similar data points, such as the human and the possum, and ask students to reason about their difference and how the graph shows the difference.

- **Do the graphs students construct match the data tables?** Students may invent many different ways to display the data they have chosen, but whatever creative ideas they try, the display should match the data. As you look at the displays students are constructing, ask them questions about the decisions they have made, such as, How did you decide to display the data this way? What are you hoping others will notice in your data? How does the data in your display match the data in the table? How did you decide on how to label your measurements? Pay attention to the relationship between the data points: Are large values large on the graph? Are small values small? And pay attention to the precise measurements to see if the values are exact.

- **How are students placing data on a graph when estimation is required?** If students have chosen to mark their vertical axis by 5s or an increment other than 1, how are they placing data that falls between these increments? Ask students questions about their reasoning to help them connect quantity to distance. For instance, on a graph with increments of 5, students should be thinking of placing 6 cm just above a line and 9 cm just below a line, whereas 7 cm and 8 cm would be in the middle.

Reflect

What features make a data display useful to the reader?

Reference

Jenkins, S. (2016). *Animals by the numbers: A book of animal infographics.* New York, NY: Houghton Mifflin Harcourt.

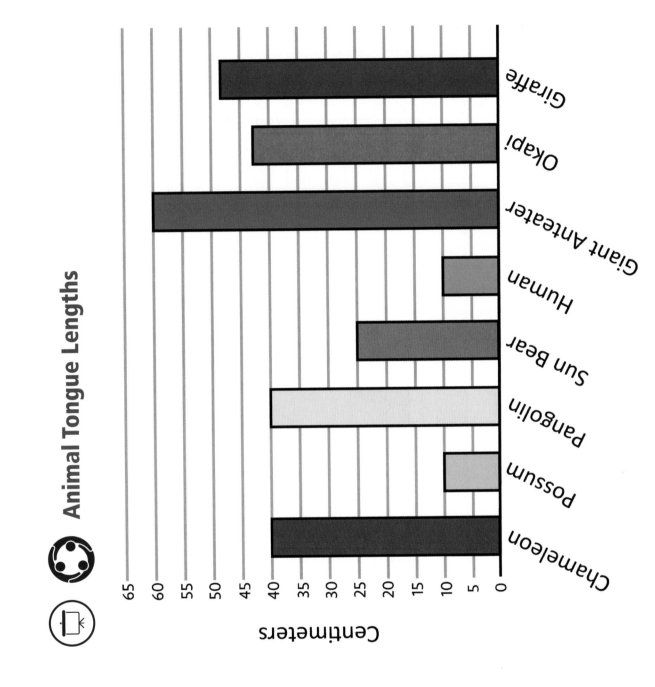

Animal Tongue Lengths

Centimeters

Chameleon · Possum · Pangolin · Sun Bear · Human · Giant Anteater · Okapi · Giraffe

65 60 55 50 45 40 35 30 25 20 15 10 5 0

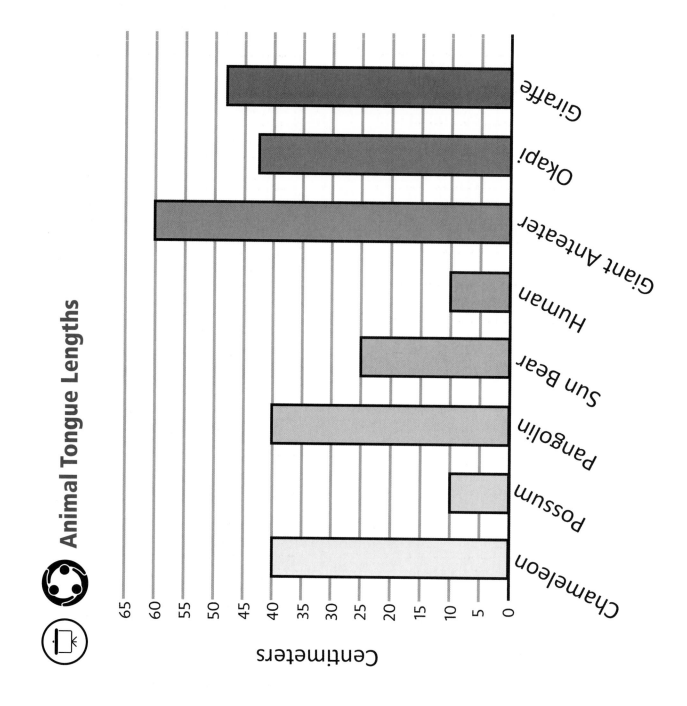

Animal Tongue Lengths

Centimeters

Animal Data Tables

Animal Tooth Lengths
(Centimeters)

Animal	Tooth Length (cm)
Tiger	8
Hippopatamus	40
Narwhal	180
Lion	10
Gorilla	2
Musk Deer	7
Great White Shark	7
Baboon	5

Animal Tail Lengths
(Centimeters)

Animal	Tail Length (cm)
Kangaroo	100
Lemur	60
Giraffe	100
Tiger	110
Alligator	200
Opossum	30
Lion	80
Red Tailed Phascogale	15

Animal Brain Weight
(Grams)

Animal	Brain Weight (g)
Dog	70
Hippopatamus	580
Lion	240
Orangutan	370
Horse	530
Camel	760
Beaver	45
Pig	180

Animal Horn Length
(Centimeters)

Animal	Horn Length (cm)
Water Buffalo	420
Rhinoceros	90
Texas Longhorn	230
Markor	150
Addax	110
Saiga	22
Mouflon	65
Giant Eland	125

Mindset Mathematics, Grade 3, copyright © 2018 by Jo Boaler, Jen Munson, Cathy Williams.
Reproduced by permission of John Wiley & Sons, Inc.

Inspector Graph-It

Snapshot

Students play with finding errors in data by looking for what doesn't make sense. Partners construct their own set of faulty data and then try to detect errors in the data displays created by the rest of the class.

Connection to CCSS
3.MD.3

Agenda

Activity	Time	Description/Prompt	Materials
Launch	10 min	Show students the Animal Height Graph and Table and discuss students' observations. Ask students to read and evaluate carefully. Sometimes there are mistakes, and we love mistakes!	Animal Height Graph and Table, to display
Explore	30 min	Partners work together to construct a faulty data set, one with both accurate and inaccurate data. Partners create a display of this data that includes a table and a graph.	• Chart paper and markers • Make available: classroom data resources, such as nonfiction books, and measurement tools
Play	15–20 min	Post students' faulty data charts. Students play Inspector Graph-It by rotating around the classroom from chart to chart trying to detect all the errors in each display. Students record the errors they find as they go.	Tools for writing while walking around the room, such as notebooks or clipboards
Discuss	15–20 min	Discuss the errors the class found hidden in each chart, and check with the authors of the chart that the class found them all. Discuss how students hunted for errors and how they had to think to construct a faulty data set.	Optional: marker or highlighter to mark errors on the charts

To the Teacher

In this activity, we encourage students to be critical of data by hunting for errors. We've created a table and graph that include two kinds of errors. First, there are places in which the graph and table do not match. Students may not be able to determine which, or if either, is correct. However, they should detect the discrepancy and conclude that some error exists. The second kind of error is one of logic. Again, students may not know the actual data, but they likely know that a hippopotamus is not a lot shorter than a tiger. When the data shows the opposite, this should arouse students' suspicion. Encourage students to develop a critical eye on data and to constantly ask, Does this make sense?

Activity

Launch

Launch the lesson by showing students the Animal Height Graph and Table on a projector. Ask students what they notice in the data. Give students a moment to turn and talk to a partner about their observations. Collect some noticings, and be sure to ask students to come up to point out where their observation or inference came from in the data. Students may notice errors at this stage, or they may not. If they do, draw attention to the error, and ask other students if they agree that it does not make sense.

Ask students to read the graph and table carefully. Sometimes there are mistakes, and we love mistakes. Remind students that we should always read graphs and tables in an inquisitive way and not just assume they are accurate. Give students another opportunity to turn and talk, this time focusing on finding errors in the data. Discuss what students notice and their reasoning behind their conclusions. Focus on the reasoning and how students know something doesn't make sense. Be sure students have attended to both kinds of errors in the data—discrepancies between the table and graph and logical errors.

Explore

Ask students to work in partners to create their own faulty data. They must create a data set, with both a table and graph, that includes some true data and some errors. The errors can be discrepancies between the table and graph, logical errors where the data doesn't make sense, or both. Partners need to first consider what kind of data they would like to display. Students can collect data in the classroom or from available resources. For instance, students could measure the heights of furniture in your classroom or use a nonfiction text to find out the speeds of land mammals. However, students should be careful that the errors they put into their data should be the kind that someone could notice by looking carefully and thinking about the data, rather than by knowing facts.

Partners construct a table and graph to show the data set on chart paper. The data should include titles and labels to make the data clear. Partners should make a list that they can keep to themselves of the errors they have hidden in the data.

Play

Post partners' data charts around the room. Each chart should also be clearly labeled with the names of the students who created it. Play Inspector Graph-It by having partners rotate around the room, taking a few minutes at each chart to try to catch the errors in the data displayed. Encourage students to be detectives and hunt down every error they can. Ask students to jot down in their notebooks or on clipboards the errors they find for each data display as they rotate. For instance, students might record that Tupa and Kia's data of animal weights has an error because a rhino is not lighter than an iguana.

Discuss

Discuss each chart, asking the class what errors they found in the data. The partners who created the chart being discussed should have out the list of errors they put into the data and check them off as the class names them. You may want to use a colored marker or highlighter to mark these errors on the charts as the class catches them. After the class has discussed all the errors they found together, ask the authors of the data set whether there were any flaws the class missed.

Discuss the following questions:

- How did you have to think about the data to catch errors?
- What kinds of errors were hardest for you to catch? Why do you think that is?
- What did you have to think about to construct the faulty data?

Look-Fors

- **Are students noticing errors of both kinds?** During the launch, you'll want to be sure students have noticed both discrepancies and logical errors in the data.

Rather than having students head off to find a resource to check each data point—a strategy that would likely identify errors but is inefficient to use regularly—support students in using what they already know to ask, Does this make sense? How are the data points related? Do those relationships make sense? How are the table and graph related? Are they consistent?

- **Are students constructing data sets that have accuracies?** In the excitement to make a fake data set, students may overlook using accurate data as well. Having both accurate and inaccurate data mixed together makes finding the errors harder, and we all like a good challenge. Be sure students are starting with an accurate set of data—for example, counts of objects in your classroom or information from a book on a topic the class is investigating in science. Then ask students how they could change the data to create errors.

- **Are students constructing data sets with errors that could be detected by other students?** When students try to be good and sneaky with their data set, they might make only very slight changes to the data, such that no one would be able to detect the error. As you talk to students while they are constructing their data sets, ask them about the errors they are putting into the data. Ask them if they think others would be able to spot the mistake using what they already know. For instance, the class should be able to figure out that a classroom chair is not 100 inches tall, but they may not be able to tell whether the chair is actually 20 or 22 inches high.

- **How are students justifying the errors they see?** When students claim they have found an error, be sure to press them to explain their reasoning. They should be able to draw on reasoning that others will understand and share. For instance, a student should be pointing to the two data points in the graph and table that should match but do not. For logical errors, students might draw on prior knowledge of the object itself (such as, "I know the table is about 2 feet tall.") or comparative knowledge (such as, "I know the table is shorter than the bookcase" or "I know the table is about half my height, and I'm 4 feet tall"). Both kinds of reasoning are valuable and should be highlighted so that others can draw on these kinds of reasoning.

Reflect

How do you know when data doesn't make sense?

Animal Height Graph and Table

Animal	Feet
Camel	10
Brown Bear	5
Ostrich	9
Elephant	11
Tiger	4
Moose	7
Hippopotamus	2
Giraffe	18

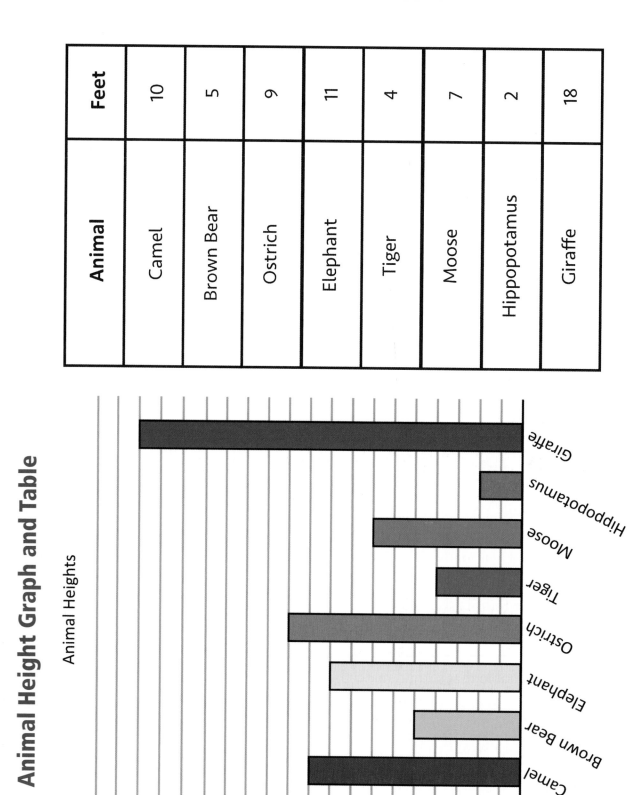

Animal Heights

Data Tells Us about Ourselves
Snapshot

What is the most common car color where you live? Students develop and try out a data collection plan to answer this question, and then look across the data collected by the whole class to see what can be learned from the similarities and differences. We offer two options for multiday extensions that put students in charge of using data to investigate their school or community.

Connection to CCSS
3.MD.3

Agenda

Activity	Time	Description/Prompt	Materials
Launch	10–15 min	Show students the Parking Lot Photo and invite observations. Ask students to predict, What is the most common car color in our area? As a class, develop a data collection plan that would help answer this question.	Parking Lot Photo, to display
Explore	30+ min	Partners work together to implement the class's data collection plan. Students develop ways to organize and display the data. Partners make observations and use their evidence to come to a conclusion, which they include on a display.	• Charts and markers • Data collection and display tools, such as clipboards, grid paper (see appendix), and tape
Discuss	20 min	Do a gallery walk of all the data and conclusions from all partnerships. Discuss the similarities and differences in the data the groups collected, and what may have led to differences. Come to a class conclusion about the most common car color in your area.	

(Continued)

Activity	Time	Description/Prompt	Materials
Extend	Varies: 2+ days	Two choices are offered for extension: investigation of a classroom- or school-based question, or the development of a community-based research project. Both require defining a question, developing a data collection plan, collecting and displaying data, and coming to a conclusion to share.	Data collection and display tools, such as clipboards, grid paper (see appendix), tape, charts, and markers

To the Teacher

In this investigation, we have approached developing the skills to use data to answer questions with a question we think any class could reasonably ask and answer with locally gathered data: What is the most common car color in your area? We aim to support students to develop a plan for collecting and examining data that helps them address the question. We encourage you to think about the ways that the physical location and resources of your school site might give students opportunities to collect data. Can you see cars driving by your classroom window? Do they go by often enough to get a real sample in a reasonable time? Does your school have a large (and, we hope, calm) parking lot? Is there parallel parking on the street in front of your school? Could you take students on a walking tour of your neighborhood to tally parked cars? We have not dictated a plan in this lesson because students should develop the plan, and it must be reasonable in your context. Thinking through the logistics of data collection in advance will help you respond to students' ideas and take up those that are safe and reasonable.

Students do not need to all use the same plan or collect data simultaneously. You might decide to break the class into smaller groups to do data collection in shifts. The differences in the data the groups collect will only add to the later whole-class discussion. Partners should be in charge of deciding how much data they need, and, to the extent that is practical, we encourage you to give students choices about how to collect the data. For instance, some students may want to just collect from one full row of the parking lot, while others want to do the back half, and still others want to try to count them all. These different choices will give your class lots to talk about in the end.

We think this initial investigation will give students many opportunities to learn about using data from the real world to answer questions, but we recognize the limitations of the specific question we've posed. Students will be far more motivated to collect and analyze data if they are attempting to answer their own questions. In the extension of this lesson, we've offered two different ideas for multiday investigations of authentic questions. Students will build on what they learn investigating the car question to pose and research their own questions. These extensions are open ended and take some planning to tailor them to the opportunities in your school and community. We think it's worth the work. Students often have data thrust at them, or gain experience with data conducting surveys of things they aren't really invested in. We think choosing one of the extension options here will give students avenues for seeing the power of data in the real world.

Activity

Launch

Launch by showing students the Parking Lot Photo and asking them what they notice. Give students a chance to turn and talk, and then take students' observations. Note that students may notice things about how the cars are arranged and the colors. Probe students to provide some evidence for their observations, particularly observations that compare (such as, "There are more white cars than orange.") or estimate (such as, "I think there are more than 100 cars there.").

Source: Image by Shutterstock.com/Aleksei Kazachok.

Pose the question, What is the most common car color in our area? Ask students to make a prediction based on the photo or what they know. Ask students to share their predictions and their reasoning. Be sure to make connections between their evidence and their prediction. For instance, students might say that they predict white is the most common because of all the white cars in the photo. You would want to make the connection clear that they are only seeing some cars, but they think that this photo represents all cars. You might ask them if they think this photo would match the cars where you live.

Ask, How could we collect data to answer this question? Tell students that you don't have a photo like this one taken where you live, so you will need a different way to collect data to answer the question. Possibilities include counting cars in the parking lot, cars parallel parked on the street in front of the school, or cars as they drive by. Work together to come up with either one shared plan for the class or a couple of possibilities that you can reasonably support.

Explore

Students work in partners to collect data following the class plan or choosing from the plans the class developed. Students need to figure out a way to record the data they collect, organizing it so they can use it to make conclusions. You may want to take students out of the building to do a walking survey of cars in a particular area, or students may be able to observe cars through the classroom window or from another indoor vantage point.

Once partners have collected what they think is enough data, they need to design a way to display the data to help answer the question, What is the most common car color in our area? Students should be encouraged to display all of their data, even the data for colors that are less popular, so that the class can make comparisons later. Their displays should include all data, their conclusion about the most popular color, and how their data supports that conclusion.

Discuss

Have students post their displays, including any graph and table data they have, their conclusions, and their supporting evidence. Do a gallery walk, in which students walk around and look at the different displays and conclusions. As they walk, student should be thinking about the following questions:

- How is our data similar?
- How is our data different? Why might our data be different?
- What appears to be the most common color in our area?

Discuss the differences and similarities in the data collected by the different groups, and ideas about why the data might not be the same. Ask students:

- What conclusions can we draw about the most common color in our area?
- What data did you find most convincing? Why?
- What other data would we want to collect to be sure?

Extend

There are two possibilities for extension, depending on what would excite your students:

1. Ask students to pose their own question about their school or community that they could reasonably collect data to answer. Note that students are often encouraged to ask questions that focus on favorites, but in this investigation, we'd like to go beyond making conclusions about what the students in one class like, toward being able to think about the school, neighborhood, or community. Work with students to generate questions that intrigue them and where data could be collected, such as:
    - How much waste is created by each grade level (or class or lunch period) at lunch?
    - Which lunches do the teachers eat? Which lunches do the kids eat?
    - How do kids get to school?
    - What do kids do after school? How does that change each day?
    - How much paper does each class recycle?
    - How much litter is left in each hallway (or in front of each classroom) each day?
    - What books are checked out each week from the library?

    Note that these are just examples, and we encourage you to brainstorm as a class. Students should make a prediction (or hypothesis) about the question and then devise a way to collect the needed data. Students will then need to create a display and a way to share. Students should make observations about their data that help answer their question or notice surprising findings. Create time for each group to share what they have found and for the class to ask questions.

2. Identify an area in your school, classroom, or community that genuinely needs research for decision making. This could be something like designing a new playground, determining what new books to order for the classroom or school library, planning for a school or classroom event (such as back-to-school night or a party), or making a recommendation to the community or town on a new project (such as putting together a softball league, planning for a community garden, or dealing with a community space that is not well cared for or used). Here the extension is more involved and more authentically similar to the work researchers do. Students need to:

- Define the question(s) that need to be explored.
- Determine how to gather data to answer those questions. Whom can we ask? Where can we find the data?
- Collect data and determine how to represent the data so that observations can be made.
- Determine what the data does and does not tell about the questions that were asked.
- Make a recommendation based on the data to support the decision making.
- Present their findings to an audience.

Although planning for and executing this extension could take considerable time, we think students would be deeply engaged in supporting an authentic decision-making process with data and recommendations.

Look-Fors

- **How are students deciding what cars to sample?** Sampling is not a concept that we typically discuss with students in elementary school, but the question we have asked about common car color is one where sampling matters. You'll likely only have access to a sample near your school, of cars either parked nearby or driving past, but students do have a choice of how many cars to sample before they decide they have enough data. Certainly, 5 or 6 cars isn't enough, and a thousand is not necessary. So, how many cars are enough for you to feel confident in your conclusion? This is a great question to be discussing with students as they collect data, and it will create useful variation among the different groups' data to discuss. The sample size is one factor that will contribute to differences among the data sets, and possibly the conclusions.

- **What categories are students using for classifying their data?** Students who use large categories, such as *blue,* will get different results from those who use finer categories, such as *light blue, navy,* and *teal.* There is no single correct way to create the categories, but consistency is valuable. If students use small categories for some of their data, they should use small categories across their data, where possible. You may want to ask students how they are deciding on the categories and whether they agree on what each category means. There are always marginal cases that need to be resolved, and partners should agree on how to categorize each car.

- **Do students' data displays match and make sense?** As we worked on in the previous activities in this big idea, different representations of the same data set should match and make sense. It would be surprising for students all to enter the same parking lot and come out with wildly conflicting data. Further, after students tally up the cars, there are lots of opportunities for inadvertent errors to creep in, from counting to recording to displaying. Ask students how they are making sure their data is accurate. Draw students' attention to any discrepancies and help them reason through how these crept in and where the accurate data most likely is.

- **How are students supporting their conclusions with evidence?** Regardless of the questions students are investigating, they need to use the data reasonably to support conclusions. Students should pick out useful parts of the data to help them address the questions asked. They also need to recognize when multiple answers are reasonable. For instance, if your car survey ends with 42 white cars and 39 blue cars, it would be difficult to claim confidently that white is the most popular, because the two values are too close to be sure. If you notice that your data yields two close leading values, draw the class's attention to what this data means, with particular emphasis on what it *could* mean. In this case, it *could* mean that blue is just as popular as white. This is where we return to the importance of the sample; this is not an election where every vote gets counted and even one vote can create a winner. Here we are getting a small slice of the real data, just a glimpse, and our conclusions need to acknowledge this. If you really want to know which is the most popular, it may mean you need to collect more data. If it is reasonable, encourage students to do just that. If, in the end, the data shows that it is too close to call, this is a conclusion that can be defended with the data.

Reflect

What kinds of questions can data help us answer? How do you decide what data to collect to answer your questions?

Parking Lot Photo

Mindset Mathematics, Grade 3, copyright © 2018 by Jo Boaler, Jen Munson, Cathy Williams. Reproduced by permission of John Wiley & Sons, Inc.

BIG IDEA 2

Thinking around Shapes

An important new finding from neuroscience highlights the value of students physically moving to learn mathematical concepts, as movement helps ideas embed and be held in the sensory motor parts of the brain. The area of research that communicates this is known as embodied cognition, and researchers in this field recommend learning mathematics through movement. In our own teaching at a Youcubed summer camp, we found that students learned difficult mathematical concepts more deeply and strongly when they learned them through movement. In this big idea, we give students opportunities to move with mathematics as they consider perimeter, a linear measurement that is often confusing and troubling for students. Later in the book, we will provide lessons on area, and our intention is to help students build a deep understanding of these two ideas that will stay with them throughout their lives.

In our Visualize activity, we ask students to explore the idea of perimeter by using a piece of string to measure around objects in their classroom. This activity not only gets students to use their arms to understand the concept of "around" but also gives them an opportunity to estimate, another mathematical concept that is important and often neglected in textbooks. Students move around the room trying to decide which objects have a distance around them that will match the length of the string they have been given. Because each group of students will have a different length of string, this will be a time for discovery, estimation, and conversation. Later, when students display their string with the drawings they have made, their brains will be making connections as visual, numerical, and spatial pathways communicate. We have included a table for students to record their mistakes as they note objects that had a distance around that was either too small or large for their string.

In our Play activity, we ask students to imagine walking around a shape. Students are introduced to a shape placed on a grid, and they are asked to imagine walking around the shape and counting the perimeter. If you have access to a square tile floor or can make a square tile area on the floor, you can invite students to physically walk and count. This is another opportunity for students to make brain connections, as counting and moving involve different areas of the brain. If you see students gesture when they are talking about their mathematical ideas, you will know that the ideas are held in the sensory motor parts of their brain. After students have studied a shape with a perimeter of 36, they will be asked to create other shapes that have the same perimeter. We are again emphasizing an opportunity for students to be creative and share their findings with their classmates. The classroom discussion ends with students looking at one another's findings and searching for patterns in their data. This is an opportunity for students to be immersed in the concept of perimeter, shapes, and pattern finding. If students are producing work that looks different from one another's, you know that mathematical creativity has been achieved!

In our Investigate activity, we encourage you to use geoboards, which are important classroom manipulatives that can be used for many different activities throughout the year. We hope you find many additional ways to use these engaging classroom manipulatives. The goal of this investigation is for students to explore irregular shapes and work to determine the characteristics of a shape that will make it have a very large perimeter. Students will explore irregular shapes on their geoboard as they work to understand the characteristics of a shape that creates a large perimeter. An important aspect of this investigation is considering what is and is not a shape. We have included a set of examples for class discussion. Together students will answer the question: What characteristics does a shape have that results in a big perimeter?

If you have time for the extension, students will have an opportunity to understand the idea of having a constraint as they explore shapes. We have included a set of constraint cards. We encourage you to let students read them first and work to make sense of their meaning. This may be a time of struggle, which is a great time to remind students of the importance of struggle for brain growth. You can also invite students to come up with their own questions and pursue their own answers to their questions. This is one of the best extensions of any math task: ask students to design their own questions and try to make them difficult! Students love to do this; it gives them responsibility and invites them to think deeply about mathematical concepts.

Jo Boaler

Get Your Arms around It

Snapshot

Students build the concept of perimeter as the "distance around" by finding objects they can surround with a piece of string, and making lots of useful mistakes along the way.

Connection to CCSS
3.MD.8

Agenda

Activity	Time	Description/Prompt	Materials
Launch	5–10 min	Ask students to make a loop with their arms and estimate an object that would just fit inside. Tell students they are going to be exploring the distance around objects. Give partners string and ask them to brainstorm classroom objects they might be able to surround with it.	Strings, one per partnership, each cut to a different length between 12 and 60 inches
Explore	20–25 min	Partners use their string to identify objects they could just surround with it. Students draw the object they identify, and record the objects that were too small or large on their Useful Mistakes note-taking sheet.	• Strings (already provided) • Blank paper for drawing • Useful Mistakes note-taking sheet, one per partnership
Discuss	15+ min	Create a class display of each partnership's string and their illustrations of the objects it surrounds. Post these from shortest to longest. Discuss what students found that surprised them and what was challenging about finding objects to surround. Name the length of the string, or distance around, as the *perimeter*.	Space for creating a class display and tools for posting students' findings

To the Teacher

Central to this activity is embodied cognition, the notion that we carry knowledge in our bodies and can develop a physical sense of things that we don't have words (yet) to describe. Oftentimes, perimeter is taught simultaneously with area, and students can get the two concepts confused. We believe that this happens for two reasons that this book is structured to address. First, by teaching two related but distinct ideas together, we blur the distinctions, and students learn the concepts muddied together. In this book, we have dedicated one big idea to perimeter and then positioned area later in the text, after work with equal groups, so that it is associated with ideas of multiplication and not tangled up with perimeter. Second, this tangling up happens because students don't have a solid concept of the physical attribute of perimeter (or area). We want students to explore perimeter as the idea of surrounding before we dig into how to calculate it. This activity is designed to build a solid sense of what it means to go around an object and support this physical experience of surrounding, or trying to surround, objects as the meaning of perimeter.

Also intertwined in this lesson are notions of visualization and estimation. Looking at a string, or a loop of arms, and imagining what will fit inside is difficult work. We don't often estimate distances around, so they are challenging for us to imagine. Students are going to make tons of mistakes as they imagine, estimate, and test objects. We encourage you to celebrate the mistakes and surprises that this lesson leads to.

For this activity, you'll need to prepare different lengths of string for each partnership. We think strings ranging from 12 to 60 inches work well for this activity, but precise measurement is not necessary. It is useful, though, for each partnership to get a different length. When choosing string, try to find something that does not stretch much. Some yarn can be pulled several inches longer, but twine or ribbon tend not to change length when pulled.

Activity

Launch

Launch this activity by asking students to stand and make a loop with their arms, with their fingers or hands touching, like a hug in the air. Ask, What could you surround with your arms? What could you *just* fit inside your arms? Take some ideas from students about the objects that they could put their arms around. If students offer any examples of objects in your classroom, you can invite them to test their ideas physically. Ask, What could you surround if you join hands with a partner? Ask students to estimate some objects, and give some students the opportunity to test their ideas in front of the group. These tests should be low stakes; celebrate the surprises that come from estimating.

Tell students that they are going to be surrounding objects today. The goal is to explore the distance around objects. Give partners a piece of string. Different partnerships should get strings of different lengths. Tell students that the string is the distance around some object. What could the object be? Ask students to turn and talk to their partner and generate some ideas that they could test today. Remind students that they can try as many ideas as they want and that they are likely to make lots of useful mistakes today.

Explore

Send partners off with their string to identify, test, and collect objects that the string just surrounds. Perfection is not important, but the string should be close to the distance around the objects students collect. Students should draw the objects that they find can be surrounded by their string. We think drawing is a productive way to record thinking and begin to grapple with proportion. Depending on your context and the length of the string, students might actually collect these objects physically, too.

Ask students to use the Useful Mistakes note-taking sheet to keep a list of objects that are too small and too large to be surrounded by their string. Keeping track of the mistakes can help students improve their estimates over time.

Discuss

After students have had the opportunity to explore lots of possibilities, bring students together to discuss the results. We suggest that a class display of the findings makes the discussion richer. Find a space, such as a bulletin board or wall, where you can post each group's string stretched horizontally along with the group's illustrations of the objects they found. Call groups up to post and share in order from shortest to longest string length.

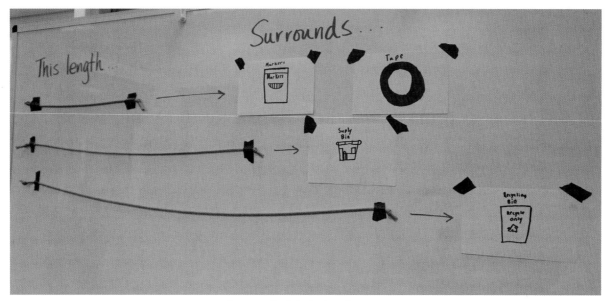

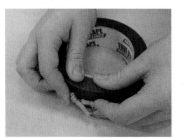

One example of sharing in a classroom

This string surrounds a roll of tape.

This string goes around the recycle bin.

This string wraps around a supply box.

Discuss the posted solutions. Ask, What do you see that surprises you? Why is it surprising? Name for students that these strings are the length around the objects, and in math we call this length the *perimeter.* Add the word *perimeter* to your class display.

Debrief students' experience looking for objects with the perimeter of their string by discussing the following questions:

- What surprised you?
- What estimates did you make that you were surprised to find didn't work?
- Did you over- or underestimate more often?
- Did you notice anything looking at your Useful Mistakes sheet that helped you?
- What makes it hard to estimate the distance around (or perimeter)?
- What did you figure out when you were trying to find objects?

Look-Fors

- **How closely does the string fit around the objects students have identified?** Perfection is certainly not the goal in this activity, but we do want the string to come close to fitting around the object. Students might also be wrapping the string around at funny angles to get it to fit better. Encourage students to go right around the object, as though giving a hug or putting on a belt. Objects are, of course, irregular. If students find that the string fits around the object vertically, rather than horizontally, or around a certain part of the object (such as the seat of the chair or the leg of the desk), then encourage them to draw the object carefully, labeling where it is that the string fits around the object.

- **How are students drawing and labeling their objects?** In the end, this is the work product and the only evidence students will have to share with the class. Furthermore, drawing encourages students to decompose three-dimensional objects into parts and think proportionally. Although this is not a lesson in drawing, you should encourage students to record their findings the best way they know how to communicate what they have discovered to others. It is worth prompting students to spend some time on their drawings so that they are clear and specific enough to be recognizable. Labels can be a useful tool in this effort.

Reflect

When might finding the perimeter of something be useful?

⬡ Useful Mistakes

Objects That Are Too Small	Objects That Are Too Large

36-Unit Walk

Snapshot

Students construct rectangles and other rectilinear shapes with a perimeter of 36 units. The class investigates patterns in shapes with the same perimeter.

Connection to CCSS
3.MD.8
3.OA.9

Agenda

Activity	Time	Description/Prompt	Materials
Launch	5–10 min	Show students the image of the Rectangular Walk and ask them how far a walk around the rectangle would be. Students turn and talk and share ways of thinking. Introduce the task.	Rectangular Walk sheet, to display
Play	20–25 min	Partners create rectangles for which a walk around the perimeter would be 36 units long. Students record their rectangles on grid paper and look for patterns.	• Grid paper (see appendix) • Square tiles
Discuss	10–15 min	Students share the rectangles they created with a perimeter of 36 units. The class works together to organize the rectangles to look for patterns and any missing solutions.	Grid paper (see appendix)
Play	20+ min	Ask students what shapes they can make with a 36-unit perimeter if the shapes no longer need to be rectangles. Partners work to construct and record shapes and explore how the patterns from rectangles can help them.	• Grid paper (see appendix) • Square tiles

(Continued)

Activity	Time	Description/Prompt	Materials
Discuss	10 min	Students share the shapes they constructed with a 36-unit perimeter, and the class discusses any patterns they notice.	
Extend	25+ min	Partners select their own perimeter and explore whether the patterns the class discovered in the 36-unit shapes hold true for other perimeters.	• Grid paper (see appendix) • Square tiles

To the Teacher

In this activity, we shift from surrounding objects to quantifying perimeter. We invite students to construct a series of shapes with the same perimeter, in this case 36 units. In making lots of mistakes, students will uncover patterns in the shapes that share a perimeter. One way of thinking about this is to notice that the length and width add to half the perimeter. So, all the rectangles with a perimeter of 36 units will have a length and width that add up to 18 units: $1 \times 17, 2 \times 16, 3 \times 15, 4 \times 14$, and so on. This would be a useful pattern for the class to discover by the end of the first discussion. But as students get started, they are likely to struggle to find the first solution. When they do struggle, we encourage you to support students in thinking about the rectangles they attempt and to ask how they could revise the rectangle to get closer to a perimeter of 36. Do they need to make the rectangle larger or smaller? How might they try this? Reasoning about the rectangles that don't work will keep students connected to the meaning of perimeter and avoid a frustrating guessing game.

The extension asks students to test the patterns they have found in this task with other perimeters. We think this is a valuable use of time, solidifying the patterns in perimeter by seeing how (and whether) they generalize.

Activity

Launch

Launch this lesson by showing students the Rectangular Walk sheet on a projector. Ask students, If you were going to take a walk around this rectangle, starting and ending at the dot, how far would your walk be? Give students a moment to turn and talk to a partner, then ask for ideas and reasoning. Let students come up and show their thinking on the screen. Be sure to trace their walk on the rectangle, either with a finger or with a color, to emphasize the perimeter as the location and length of the walk. Label any counting or adding work students did to arrive at the distance of the walk.

Tell students that today they will be taking a walk around another rectangle. The walk is 36 units long, and their job is to figure out what the rectangle could look like.

Play

Provide students grid paper (see appendix) to record their thinking. Offer square tiles for students to build rectangles with, but make sure they are attending to the distance around, or perimeter, rather than the number of tiles. Ask students to work in partners to come up with as many rectangles as they can with a distance around, or perimeter, of 36 units. For each rectangle they find, partners record and label it on the grid paper. Encourage students to label the side lengths and provide a number-sentence label that could be used to find the length of the walk around the shape.

If students think they have found all the possible solutions, ask them to look at the rectangles they found. Ask, What patterns do you notice?

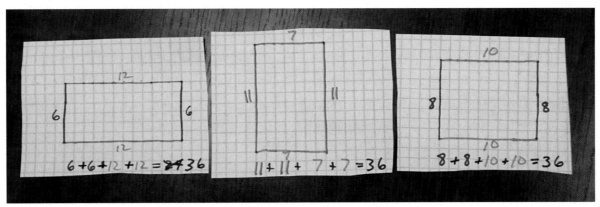

Student work that is cut and ready to sort

Discuss

Invite students to share their solutions. For each rectangle, record it on grid paper (see appendix) with labels. Leave some margin between the shapes so that after students share all of the solutions they have found, you can cut out the rectangles for sorting or arranging. You need not cut the shapes perfectly around the edges; rather, you simply need to separate them so they can be moved and ordered.

Ask students, What patterns do you notice? Invite students to move the solutions around on the document camera to see relationships or organize. If students have not found all the possible solutions, this process might lead them to see what is missing. If so, be sure to discuss what patterns the students are using to identify missing solutions.

Play

Open up the solution space by asking, What if the shape did not have to be a rectangle? What solutions can you find now? Tell students that they must use the grid lines, or edges of the square tiles, in order to count the perimeter. Students work in partners to generate and record possibilities on grid paper (see appendix). For each solution students find, ask them to cut it out as you did with the rectangles—not around the perimeter, but just separating it from the larger paper. Encourage students to think about how the patterns they uncovered in the rectangles could help them in making other shapes.

Discuss

Invite partners to share solutions on the document camera, proving the perimeter. Ask students to post their solutions on a board or wall so that the class can see all that was created. Then discuss the following questions about the shapes with a perimeter of 36 units:

- What do you notice?
- What changed when we were no longer looking for rectangles? How did you use the patterns in the rectangles to help you create new shapes?
- Do you see any patterns?

Extend

Partners choose their own perimeter and try to use the patterns they noticed in the 36-unit walk to generate shapes with the perimeter they chose. Students explore the following questions:

- Are the same patterns true with a different perimeter? Why or why not?
- Do you notice anything new?

Look-Fors

- **Are students attending to the distance around the rectangles they build?** As students begin building, the easiest attribute to count is the square units that make up the area, either the tiles they are using to build or the squares on their grid paper. But to count these is to focus on area, or how much space is covered by the rectangle, rather than its perimeter. Be on the lookout for students who begin by counting out 36 square tiles. Ask probing questions about how these tiles are connected to the distance around the rectangle students will build. Students may believe that if they use 36 square tiles, they will get a perimeter of 36 units. Allow students to test this theory and reason about the results, before encouraging them to try a different strategy.

- **How are students counting the perimeter?** The perimeter is hard to count for the simple reason that it is difficult to put your finger on each line segment or tile edge to count. Sometimes students struggle to count at the corners because they require counting one tile twice. Other students may count the square tiles that form the frame around the rectangle, either inside or outside the rectangle's edges, rather than the edges themselves. You will need to watch carefully and ask questions to see exactly how students are counting, so that you can support them in counting the edges accurately.

- **How are students using their incorrect attempts to help them find solutions?** When students first make a rectangle and count its perimeter, they will likely not have made one with a perimeter of 36 units. However, this attempt can generate useful information for making a better guess. Before students push aside the square tiles or erase their drawing, ask them to reflect on this attempt and what clues it gives them for the next try. For instance, you might ask, How close to a perimeter of 36 units is it? Is it too large or too small? What could you do to this rectangle to make the perimeter closer to 36 units?

Reflect

How do we find the perimeter of a shape?

Rectangular Walk

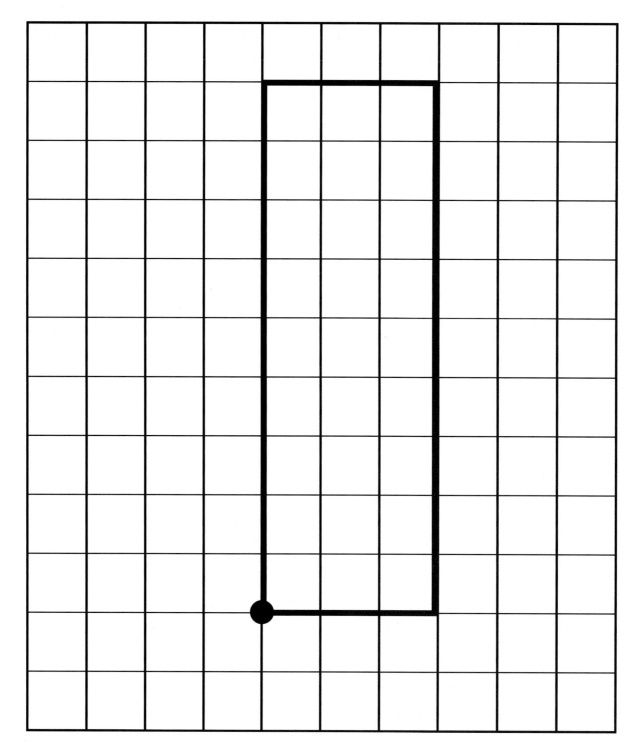

Shapes on a Plane

Snapshot

On geoboards, students try to construct the shape with the longest perimeter possible, and explore how to find the perimeters of irregular shapes.

Connection to CCSS
3.MD.8
3.MD.4

Agenda

Activity	Time	Description/Prompt	Materials
Launch	15 min	Develop a way to find the perimeter of an irregular shape on the geoboard using string and a measuring tool.	• Geoboard and rubber band • String • Meter stick or yardstick • Shape and Not a Shape sheet, to display
Explore	20–30 min	Students investigate what shape on the geoboard has the longest possible perimeter. Partners construct shapes on the geoboard, find their perimeters, and record their findings.	• Geoboard, rubber bands, meter stick or yardstick, and string, for each partnership • Geoboard Sheets, multiple copies per partnership
Discuss	15 min	Partners share the shape with the longest perimeter they made and prove its perimeter. Discuss the strategies students used for making shapes with longer perimeters and whether students think a shape with an even longer perimeter is possible.	Partners' geoboards with perimeter labels

(Continued)

Activity	Time	Description/Prompt	Materials
Extend	30+ min	Partners choose from four constraints and investigate, under the constraint, what the longest possible perimeter is for a shape on the geoboard.	• Thinking around Shapes Constraint Cards, multiple copies, cut out for students to choose from • Geoboard, rubber bands, meter stick or yardstick, and string, for each partnership • Geoboard Recording Sheets, multiple copies per partnership

To the Teacher

For this investigation, it is crucial that the class have a shared definition of a shape. We have selected polygons to be the definition of a shape, which means that the shapes have straight sides, are closed, and do not have crossed sides. Straight sides and closed figures are inevitable when making figures on the geoboard with rubber bands. However, students will likely want to make shapes with crossed sides as they try to increase the perimeter. We have provided examples and nonexamples of shapes for this activity for you to use to come to a class agreement about what counts as a shape.

Geoboards do come in different sizes, typically either 5 × 5 or 7 × 7. To account for these differences, we've provided two different kinds of recording sheets. Be sure to use the size that matches your geoboards and that all of your students use the same size of geoboard.

Activity

Launch

Launch the lesson by showing students an irregular polygon displayed on a geoboard using a rubber band, like the one shown here.

Ask students, How could we figure out how long the perimeter of this shape is? Give students a moment to turn and talk to a partner about ways they might find the

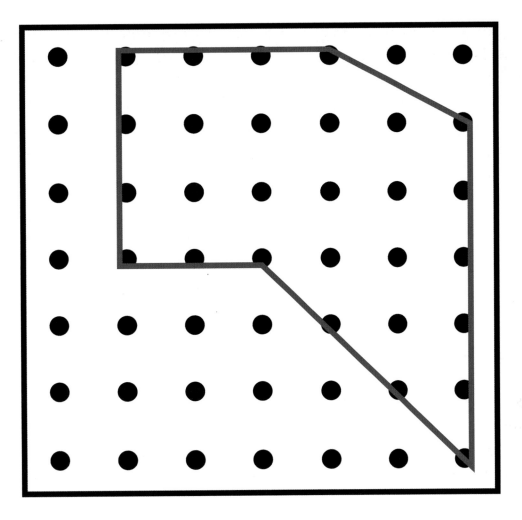

perimeter of this irregular shape. Invite students to share some ideas. Students might suggest counting, as they did in the Play activity; if so, push them to describe what they would count. On the geoboard, what could be counted is not clear, and shapes with non-right angles make this even trickier. Some students might suggest using string, as in the Visualize activity; if so, take up this idea and ask how they could make it work.

If no one suggests using string, show students some string and a meter stick or yardstick. Ask, How could these tools help us find the perimeter? Together with students, develop a method based on what they have done before. Invite students to come up to the geoboard and try using the string to find the distance around. Students will likely need extra hands to make this work.

Tell students that today they're going to investigate shapes that can be made on the geoboard and ask, What shape can we make on the geoboard that has the longest perimeter possible?

Before sending students off to get started on this investigation, come to some agreements about what is and is not a shape in this activity. Show students the Shape and Not a Shape sheet on the projector. Ask students to look at what is and is not a shape. Then ask students to turn and talk to a partner about what makes a shape for this activity. Ask for students' observations, and be sure that students noticed that shapes with crossed sides are not considered shapes in this activity.

Explore

Partners try to construct the shape on the geoboard with the longest perimeter possible. Provide partners with a geoboard, some rubber bands, string, a meter stick or yardstick, and Geoboard Sheets. Students investigate the shapes they can make, how to change the perimeter by altering the shape, and how to measure the perimeter of the shapes they have made. Partners record each shape they make on the recording sheet along with its perimeter on the geoboard.

As a class, agree on a unit of measure. We recommend either inches or centimeters. This shared unit will make it easier to compare results during the discussion.

Discuss

Before beginning the class discussion, ask partners to create on their geoboard the shape with the longest perimeter they found during the investigation. Then ask students to display their geoboard along with a label with the shape's perimeter. You might have students place these on the ledge of your whiteboard, jotting the perimeter above it on the board, or have students place them on their tables and use a sticky note next to it to label the perimeter. Regardless of the method you choose, give students a chance to look at all the possibilities. Ask a few partnerships to show how they found the perimeter of their shape; you'll particularly want the group that created the shape with the longest perimeter to prove the measurement.

Then discuss the process students went through in this investigation:

- How did you make the perimeter longer? What strategies worked?
- What makes perimeter longer? What makes perimeter shorter?
- Do you think we could make a shape with an even longer perimeter than the ones we found? How would we do it? Or why not?

Extend

Present students with the choice of a constraint. What is the shape with the longest perimeter that can be made on the geoboard, if

- The shape can have no more than six vertices?
- The shape can only have right angles?
- The shape may not include acute angles?
- The shape can only be positioned on half of the geoboard?

Provide students with these options on the Thinking around Shapes Constraint Cards so that they can choose one to try. Regardless of the constraint partners choose, students again use Geoboard Sheets to record the shapes they make, and measure all the figures they make using string and a meter stick or yardstick, labeling each shape with its perimeter. Provide time for students to share and compare findings.

Look-Fors

- **How are students measuring the perimeter?** Measuring perimeter with a string is difficult, and we do expect some degree of error as students wind it around the board and transfer the string to the meter stick or yardstick. Students should, though, be attending to how they get the string to match the sides of their figure and not slip off and change shape. They may find that they benefit from marking the string with a ruler at the start and stop places to make transferring it to the ruler easier. Alternatively, they may find that they need to use all four hands to manage the process. Encourage them to be creative in finding ways to measure as accurately as they can.
- **How are students adjusting their shapes to make the perimeter longer?** As in the Play activity, support students in using any attempt as a starting place for future ideas. Encourage students to think about how they could make the perimeter of the shape even longer. You might ask, What is one thing you could change about the shape to make the perimeter longer? Once they have revised one or more features, push students to measure and see how much longer the perimeter is. This process not only can lead to shapes with longer perimeters but also can help students develop a sense of what features make a longer perimeter.

Reflect

What kinds of shapes have a long perimeter? Why?

Shape and Not a Shape

Shapes	Not Shapes

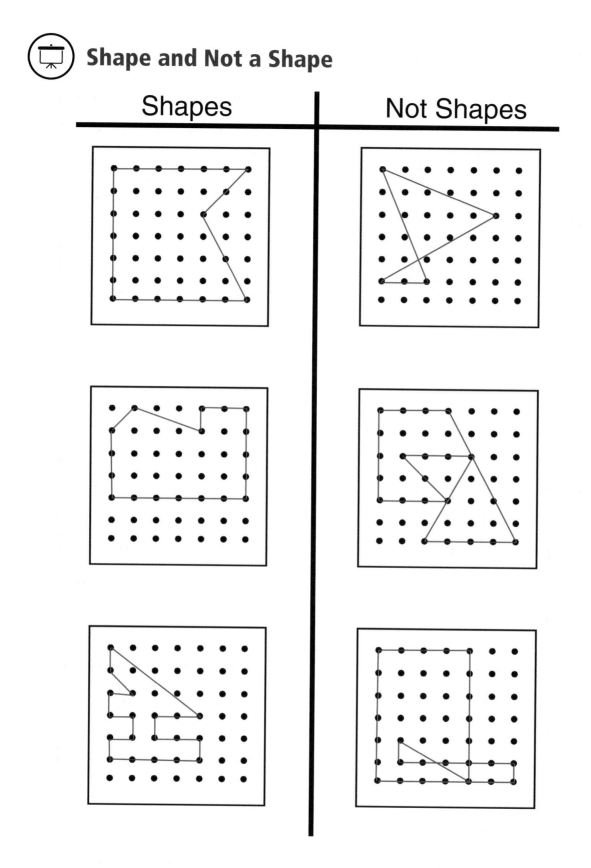

Geoboard Recording Sheet

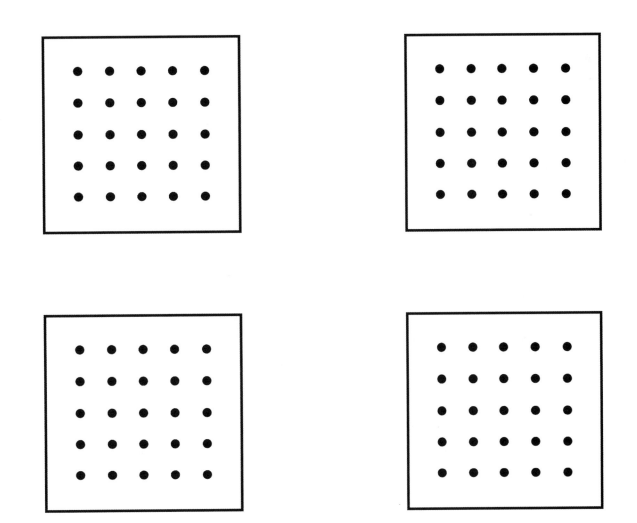

Geoboard Recording Sheet

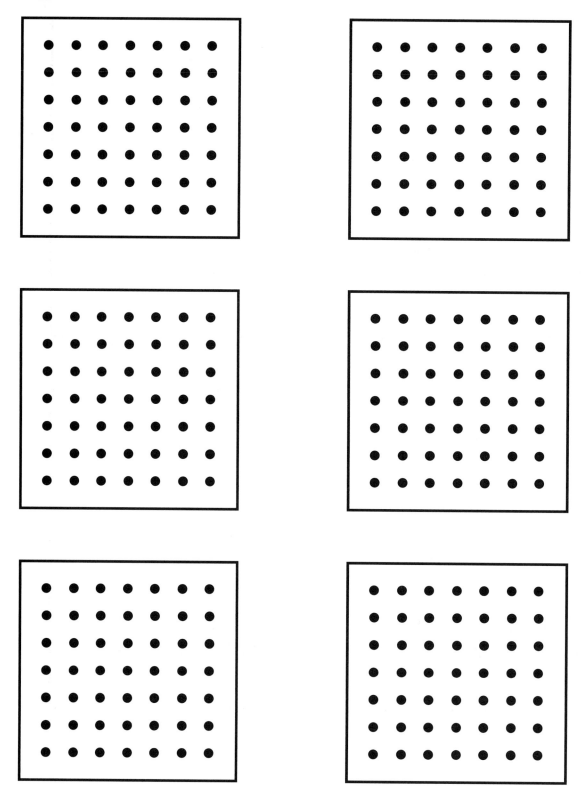

Mindset Mathematics, Grade 3, copyright © 2018 by Jo Boaler, Jen Munson, Cathy Williams.
Reproduced by permission of John Wiley & Sons, Inc.

1

Make a shape on your geoboard with the longest possible perimeter.

The shape can have up to 6 vertices.

2

Make a shape on your geoboard with the longest possible perimeter.

The shape can only have right angles.

3

Make a shape on your geoboard with the longest possible perimeter.

The shape cannot have any acute angles.

4

Make a shape on your geoboard with the longest possible perimeter.

The shape can only be on **half** the geoboard.

Thinking in Equal Groups

This big idea is focused on equal groups—a very important idea in mathematics. Gray and Tall (1994) are two researchers who worked with groups of students ages 7–13 who had been nominated by their teachers as being low-, average-, or high-achieving. The researchers asked the students number questions and collected their strategies. The researchers discovered something very important: they found that the difference between the high- and low-achieving students was not that high-achieving students knew more but that they engaged in number flexibility. When faced with an addition question, these students would break numbers apart and make friendlier numbers—for example, instead of adding 19 and 6, they added 20 and 5. This kind of number flexibility is extremely important, but when students are trained to memorize math facts blindly and work with algorithms before they understand them, they often lose the motivation to think of numbers flexibly and instead resort to memorization. This often leads them to see mathematics as a subject of memorization rather than a subject of flexibility and creative ideas. As students work on the activities in this big idea, some of them will draw on memorized math facts; that is fine, but it is not the goal of the activities. The goal is for students to think about numbers deeply, to engage with them flexibly, and to see numbers visually. Later in the book, students will work with multiplication and division, but before they do that, we invite them to encounter and deeply understand foundational mathematical concepts.

In our Visualize activity, we again visit the wonderfully flexible number 36. Students are first asked to work out the different ways they can share 36 crackers with different numbers of friends. This question may look like a traditional division question, but it differs in an important way. Instead of focusing on a single correct answer, it focuses on difference and variety. We ask students to find all of the possible solutions in this activity, hoping that some of them will think about fractions of a cracker. We encourage you to embrace students' different questions, answers, and creative thinking. When encouraged to think openly, students will come up with amazing ideas and perhaps even question the idea of infinity. The question also differs from a more typical mathematics question in that it has many different solutions, providing a time for teachers to reflect publicly on this; mathematics is a subject where there are often different solutions, something that may surprise students.

In our Play activity, we provide an image of dice and ask students to determine the number of dots. When students group dots to work out the number, they use a part of the brain called the approximate number system (ANS), and the extent to which the ANS is developed has been shown to be an important predictor of future mathematics achievement. We hope that when students see a large number of dots, they will explore different ways of grouping the dice. Celebrate the students' different solutions by giving them the students' names—for example, this is Jose's method. As students discuss the different methods, they can repeat the names of their classmates who created them, adding to the sense of mathematical community in the room. Another important strategy you can bring in with this activity is color coding—asking students to group the dots with different colors. The different colors then highlight something mathematically important. It can also be fun and engaging if students think of descriptions that go along with their method—for example, I thought of this as a herds-of-cattle approach, or the spots on a ladybug.

In our Investigate activity, we ask students to think about the operations of addition and multiplication at the same time. Students explore patterns as they take a number and study the two numbers that sum to that number and the new number that is the product of those same two numbers. Students will be collecting different number pairs and may need to work out how to organize their findings well. In my own teaching, I have found that students can often generate data, but they miss seeing important patterns because they do not know how to organize and represent their findings. I encourage you to first see what students can do. After they have worked for a while, you can drop in how to make and use a table if needed. Waiting for students to struggle before you teach a concept is an effective strategy because students understand more deeply if they see a need for a new idea, rather than being taught the idea before they encounter any need for it. When students develop "intellectual need," they learn more deeply, and when we provide students with an activity and then later show them a method or idea that they need, their learning stems from a place of intellectual need, and their brains are primed to learn the new idea well.

Jo Boaler

Reference

Gray, E., & Tall, D. (1994). Duality, ambiguity, and flexibility: A "proceptual" view of simple arithmetic. *Journal for Research in Mathematics Education, 25*(2), 116–140.

Sharing Crackers
Snapshot

There are 36 crackers to be shared equally for snack. Partners explore how many kids can share the crackers and how many crackers each friend will get, building an understanding of equal groups, division, and multiplication.

Connection to CCSS
3.OA.1, 3.OA.2, 3.OA.3, 3.OA.4, 3.OA.5, 3.OA.6

Agenda

Activity	Time	Description/Prompt	Materials
Launch	5–10 min	Show students 36 square tiles and tell students that these represent crackers that need to be shared equally for snack. Pose the questions, How many kids can share? How many crackers will each kid get?	36 square tiles (or crackers), to display
Explore	20–30 min	Partners work together using tiles to find as many solutions as possible for sharing the crackers equally. Students record their solutions in notebooks or on blank paper using numbers and pictures as evidence.	36 square tiles per partnership, in a bowl or container
Discuss	15+ min	Partners share the solutions they found. Record students' solutions in a table on one chart and their strategies on a second chart. Ask students if they think the class has found all possible solutions.	Charts and markers
Explore	15–20 min	Partners reorganize the table of solutions to look for patterns and find any missing solutions.	The Sharing Crackers Organizer, one per partnership

Activity	Time	Description/Prompt	Materials
Discuss	10–15 min	Discuss the patterns students noticed and whether they think the class has now found all the possible solutions. Label the work students have been engaged in to break the crackers into equal-size groups as *division*. If students have built up equal groups, name this as *multiplication*.	
Extend	20–30 min	Partners test the patterns they found with a different number of crackers.	Square tiles, for each partnership

To the Teacher

This is an open-ended task that initially sounds like a closed task. Students may hear this problem and assume that there can be only one answer, but then get stuck because there is not enough information to find that one correct answer. We encourage you to invest time during the launch making it clear to students that there are many possible solutions to this problem and that they are in charge of figuring out two things: how many kids can share and how many crackers each kid will get.

We intend this task to be an opportunity to work with equal groups and build a solid conceptual foundation for division, multiplication, and the relationship between the two. This foundation is far more solid if students first have the opportunity to solve the problem, grounded in the crackers and sharing, and then at the end the class learns the names for the work they have already done. Some students may have experience with multiplication or division before this task; encourage them to use these ideas while connecting them back to the crackers and kids in the problem.

The problem also brings up the possibility for students to see the commutative property of multiplication. It is an important conjecture to have students test when they first begin to see that, for instance, if 2 kids get 18 crackers each, then 18 kids can get 2 crackers each. Rather than just confirming for students that this always works, invite them to explore whether it is always true and share their results with the class during the next discussion. It is not intuitive that this relationship exists, because 2 kids with 18 crackers each is very different from 18 kids with 2 crackers each.

Activity

Launch

Show students 36 square tiles or crackers on a document camera. Tell students that these represent 36 crackers that can be shared for a snack, and that we want to share the crackers equally. Their job today is to work with a partner to figure out how many kids can share the crackers and how many crackers each kid will get. Point out that there are many, many answers to this task and that students should try to solve the problem as many different ways as they can, showing all of their thinking in their notebooks or on blank paper.

Explore

Provide partners with a bowl or container with 36 square tiles (or crackers) inside. Student work in pairs to answer two questions:

- How many kids can share the crackers?
- How many crackers will each kid get?

Partners develop ways to record each solution they find, using both pictures and numbers. Encourage students to record their attempts that they find do not work, showing in their recording why what they tried did not lead to equal shares.

Discuss

Discuss the solutions students found. Organize solutions into a table with columns labeled Number of Crackers, How Many Kids Can Share? and How Many Crackers Will Each Kid Get?

Record on a separate chart the strategies students used, such as passing out the tiles, using what they know about numbers, and doubling and halving.

After you have collected all of the solutions the class found, ask students, Do you think we have found all the ways of sharing that are possible with these 36 crackers? Why or why not?

Explore

Students explore these questions:

- What patterns do you notice in the solutions we found?
- How could we organize what we've found to see patterns?

Partners reorganize the table to help them see patterns. Provide students with copies of the Sharing Crackers Organizer; alternatively, students may prefer to record the different solutions on index cards or sticky notes that they can move around to organize.

If, while organizing and looking for patterns, students find new solutions, encourage them to add these new solutions to the class chart for all students to use and explore.

Discuss

Gather the class together and discuss the following questions:

- What patterns did you notice?
- How did you organize what you've found?
- Have we found all the solutions? How do you know?

As you discuss the patterns partners noticed, be sure to invite them to share on the document camera the ways they organized their tables, if possible.

When students discuss the patterns they notice and the strategies they have used, take this opportunity to name for students that what they have been doing—breaking a large group into smaller equal-size groups—is *division*. Some students will have used *multiplication* to help them by making equal groups to build up to the total. If students themselves do not yet have the language to describe these concepts, this is a prime moment for you to label them clearly. If both multiplication and division come up in the discussion, be sure to highlight how they are related and can both be used to think about making equal groups.

Extend

Ask students to test the patterns they have found with a different number of crackers, such as 24, 32, or 48. Partners explore the questions, How many different ways can the crackers be shared? How do you know when you've found all the ways?

Look-Fors

- **How are students getting started?** Students may get stuck if they do not understand that multiple solutions are possible. Given that there are few constraints, students may not know how to get started. You might ask students just to simulate sharing the crackers in their partnership and see what happens. This gets student thinking about how they might make two equal groups with their partner, which can spur them to develop a strategy such as passing the cracker out or counting and cutting in half. Once students have one solution and a strategy, you might say, What's another way you can share the crackers?

- **How are students recording and organizing their thinking?** Students may focus on using the tiles and record very little or nothing of their thinking. Prompt partners to think about how they are going to capture their thinking on the page before they put all the tiles into new groups. They might draw the groups of tiles, use numbers to label, or even use number sentences as evidence. These recordings can take up a lot of space, so encourage students to find ways to separate their different solutions. Prompt students to use labels to indicate the numbers that represent crackers and those that represent kids.

- **Are students noticing relationships or beginning to think systematically?** As you watch students work, be sure to draw their attention to the ways students are thinking about their solutions to generate new solutions. For instance, students may notice and use the commutative property, or turnaround facts, to turn the solution of 4 kids with 9 crackers each into 9 kids with 4 crackers each. Students might use a doubling and halving pattern to move from 2 kids with 18 crackers each to 4 kids with 9 crackers each. Each of these is useful in tracking down new solutions and looking for possible missing solutions. Further, these patterns apply to all multiplication and division relationships and are worth testing, sharing, and discussing. Be sure to ask students to explore whether these patterns always work, and why.

- **Are any students thinking with fractions?** Some students may become fascinated by doubling and halving and end up moving beyond whole numbers into fractions. Although working with fractions is not the intent of the lesson, we encourage you to allow this exploration. Students may start with sharing the crackers with 2 kids and getting 18 crackers each, then halve the size of each group to get 4 groups of 9 crackers. At this point many groups will stop, seeing that 9 crackers cannot be cut in half and give a whole number of crackers in each group. But other students will interpret that crackers can be cut in half, so 8 kids can each get $4\frac{1}{2}$ crackers. They might pursue this doubling and halving, cutting the crackers into smaller and smaller pieces. Provided that the students can explain what they are doing and why it makes sense, let them explore. However, when you construct your class table of solutions, make one table for whole-number solutions and keep fractional solutions on a separate chart. When the class moves to organizing solutions, ask them to focus only on the whole-number combinations.

Reflect

What is division?

 # Sharing Crackers Organizer

Number of Crackers	How Many Kids Can Share?	How Many Crackers Will Each Kid Get?

Dozens of Dice

Snapshot

Students develop strategies for counting equal groups by rolling many dice and counting the dots. The class connects these strategies to multiplication.

> **Connection to CCSS**
> 3.OA.1
> 3.OA.3

Agenda

Activity	Time	Description/Prompt	Materials
Launch	5–10 min	Show students the Dozens of Dice image and ask students, How could you figure out how many dots there are?	Dozens of Dice image, to display
Play	20+ min	Partnerships work with a collection of dice to roll them and develop ways of counting all of the dots, without counting them by ones. Students record their strategies and how they decided what strategies to use when they rolled.	Dice, 12–25 per partnership
Discuss	10–15 min	Discuss the strategies for counting the dots that student developed and how they decided which strategies to use. Name counting equal groups, repeated addition, and skip counting as *multiplication*.	• Dice, 12–25 • Chart and markers, for recording strategies
Extend	20 min	Students apply the strategies they developed to the count the dots in the Dozens of Dice image. Discuss what strategies worked best and how it was different counting when they could not move or sort the dice.	Dozens of Dice image, one for each partnership

To the Teacher

This activity makes use of the friendly equal groups students have been encountering on dice for years. Because of the useful structure of the dice, students find it easy to tell how many dots are on a single die, but finding the total number of dots on a large number of dice makes using equal groups to skip-count, and ultimately multiply, a more efficient route than counting each individual dot. You will need a large number of dice for this activity, 12–25 dice per partnership. Dice are wonderful manipulatives that we think are underused in math classrooms, particularly now that probability concepts are introduced in middle school. If this number of dice is challenging to gather, you can form larger groups of three or four students to play, or rotate partnerships through using the dice you have. Because sorting the dice physically is such a useful strategy, there is no substitution for having the actual dice for students to roll and manipulate.

If students have not yet had exposure to multiplication, this lesson can serve as an introduction to the concept of multiplication as repeated addition or as adding equal groups. Be sure to use these different ways of describing multiplication and the different symbolic ways of representing them interchangeably to help students see the connection between these different ideas. For instance, one student may see what they have done as skip counting, while another calls it addition. You can make the connection between these two ways of seeing and recording counting, while also naming that another way to think about this is *multiplication*. Layering these meanings and representations together will support students in learning about multiplication through its meaning rather than as a rote procedure.

Activity

Launch

Launch the lesson by showing students the illustrated version of the Dozens of Dice image. Ask students, How many dots are there? How could we figure it out?

There are 35 dice. How many dots are there?

Give students a moment to turn and talk to a partner about how they might figure out the number of dots in this picture. Collect student ideas and draw students' attention to ideas that use the groups of dots to help count, rather than counting dots individually. Tell students that today they are going to be developing a way to count the dots in a large group of dice.

Play

Provide each partnership with 12–25 dice. Students roll their dice and develop ways to figure out the total number of dots displayed. Students can roll their dice repeatedly to test and refine their strategies. Encourage students to move their dice around to sort, make groups, or organize to make the counting easier or more efficient. Students should create some way of recording their strategies and systems. Partners should come back to the discussion with strategies or patterns that make counting the dots efficient.

Discuss

Have a set of dice ready on a document camera or on the carpet to use as a place for students to show their strategies. Discuss the following questions, and record students' strategies on a chart:

- How did you count the dots? What strategies did you develop?
- What strategies made counting efficient?
- How did you use the groups of dots on the dice to count?

Draw students' attention to strategies that use grouping and skip counting to make counting more efficient. Name for students that when we repeatedly add groups of the same size, we call it *multiplication*. Record this term on your chart, connecting it to an example of repeated addition. You might use this opportunity to show the symbol used to represent multiplication alongside a repeated addition equation. For instance, if someone added $4 + 4 + 4 + 4 + 4 = 20$, record underneath, $4 \times 5 = 20$ and "5 groups of 4 equal 20."

Extend

Provide partners with the graphic Dozens of Dice image. Ask students to try their strategies, or those they heard others share, with the image as they try to answer the question, How many dots are there? Compare students' findings. Discuss the questions, Which strategies made the counting most accurate and efficient? How was counting different when you could not move the dice?

Look-Fors

- **Are students counting the dots by 1s?** Students may be tempted to count dots individually, knowing that they can arrive at an accurate answer this way. However, in this activity, the goal is to develop ways that don't require counting each individual dot. Encourage students to think about parts of their collection of dice that don't need to be counted one by one. For instance, students may quickly recognize that if they sort out the 2s or the 5s, they can then can skip-count these fluidly. The challenge then is, How can you use this same idea to help with the 3s, 4s, and 6s? Additional tools, such as 100s charts or number lines, may prove useful for counting by 3s, 4s, and 6s. Students might also find that decomposing the 4s and 6s into pairs (two or three sets of 2) makes counting by 2s a strategy that they can extend.

- **How are students grouping dice to count the dots?** Students will likely focus on two features: making 10s (such as pairing 4 and 6) or 5s (2 and 3), and using equal groups on the dice to skip-count (such as counting all the fours: 4, 8, 12, 16 . . .). Both kinds of composing are useful. Some strategies are more useful in some situations. For instance, if students have two 2s and six 3s, they may want to match up the pair of 2s with a pair of 3s to make 10 and then skip-count the remaining 3s. Or they may decide that making 5s isn't efficient when there is such an imbalance of 2s and 3s, and that skip-counting all of them is a better strategy. Encourage students to record the strategies they use and to think about when they choose to use one strategy over another, or how they make decisions about combining strategies.

- **Are students physically sorting the dice?** Seeing the vast collection of dice rolled haphazardly across a surface can make organizing for counting seem challenging. Students will see more patterns that they can use to develop counting strategies if they sort the dice in some way. Encourage students to move the dice around to see what they have and to make groups that they can count with confidence. You might ask, How can you move these dice around to make it easier to see how many you have?

Reflect

How are equal groups related to multiplication?

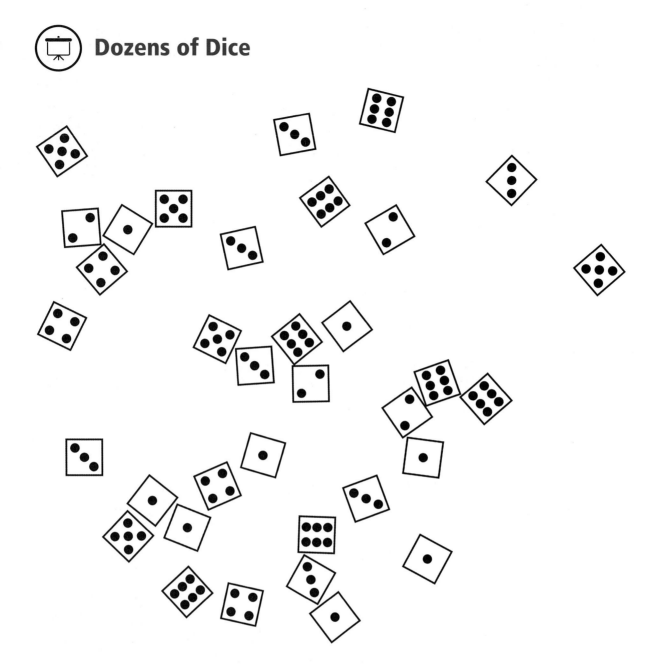

Playing with Pairs

Snapshot

Students develop ways of illustrating multiplication and look for patterns that emerge while investigating the puzzle: Two numbers add up to 10. What might you get if you multiply these numbers?

> **Connection to CCSS**
> 3.OA.1, 3.OA.5, 3.OA.9

Agenda

Activity	Time	Description/Prompt	Materials
Launch	5–10 min	Show students the puzzle: Two numbers add up to 10. What might you get if you multiply these numbers? Ask students what this might mean and how they might represent multiplying two numbers.	Playing with Pairs task page, to display
Explore	25–30 min	Partners investigate the puzzle and develop ways to illustrate multiplication using manipulatives and pictures, and record their findings on a chart. Partners look for patterns in their solutions.	• Chart and markers, for each partnership • Make available: square tiles, dice, or other manipulatives
Discuss	15–20 min	Post students' charts and invite the class to look at everyone's findings. Discuss the solutions students found and their ways of illustrating. As a class, come up with a way to organize the findings and look for patterns. Generate conjectures based on these patterns.	• Students' charts, posted around the classroom • Two charts and markers, for organizing the class's findings

(Continued)

Activity	Time	Description/Prompt	Materials
Explore	20–30 min	Partners choose a sum other than 10 and investigate the class's conjectures to find out which are always true, and which are true only sometimes. They collect their findings on a chart to share.	• Chart and markers, for each partnership • Make available: square tiles, dice, or other manipulatives • Class conjectures chart
Discuss	15 min	Post partners' charts and give students time to look at the different findings. Discuss which patterns are always true, and modify the conjectures based on this new evidence.	• Students' charts, posted around the classroom • Class conjectures chart • Markers

To the Teacher

This investigation is designed to enable students to work on representing equal groups as they explore what products can be made by numbers that add to the same sum. Students can build on the ways they developed to represent equal groups in the Sharing Crackers activity or use the arrangements of dots on dice as starting points for creating methods for representing equal groups in this investigation. Encourage students to make clear and labeled illustrations of the products they find.

The next challenge in this activity is to look for patterns in the products of numbers that add to 10, or to any shared number. Patterns are easier to see if students organize their findings. After they generate their own ideas and look at the solutions others found, encourage students to find ways to organize these findings to look for patterns, such as the table shown here.

Sum of 10	Product
0 + 10	$0 \times 10 = 0$
1 + 9	$1 \times 9 = 9$
2 + 8	$2 \times 8 = 16$
3 + 7	$3 \times 7 = 21$
4 + 6	$4 \times 6 = 24$
5 + 5	$5 \times 5 = 25$
6 + 4	$6 \times 4 = 24$
7 + 3	$7 \times 3 = 21$
8 + 2	$8 \times 2 = 16$
9 + 1	$9 \times 1 = 9$
10 + 0	$10 \times 0 = 0$

There are many patterns that students may observe in this table. Students may notice the symmetry of the table, which comes from the commutative property of multiplication. They may also notice that the products grow larger, until the middle of the table, where the product peaks, and then fall back to 0. Students might notice that the products begin and end with 0. They may notice that the products in the center of the table are close to one another, while the products at the ends are far apart. Students may see that the greatest product is the one made by 5×5, where the two factors are the same. Students may notice other patterns, too. Use these patterns to develop conjectures about what patterns might always exist when we look for the products of numbers that add to the same value, and then ask students to test these conjectures with sums other than 10.

Activity

Launch

Launch this activity by telling students that today they are going to be investigating a puzzle. Show the Playing with Pairs task page on the projector and read: Two numbers add up to 10. What might you get if you multiply these numbers?

Ask students to turn and talk to a partner: What does this task mean? Can you think of an example? Collect student interpretations of the task and one example. Make sure students understand the task and its constraints. Tell students they will need to prove their *products,* or the solutions they find when multiplying. Students should consider the question, What could you draw to represent your thinking? Give students another chance to turn and talk to a partner about what they could draw to show the result of multiplying two numbers.

Explore

Ask students in partners to generate as many different ways of solving this puzzle as possible: Two numbers add up to 10. What might you get if you multiply these numbers? Make available manipulatives for modeling this problem, such as square tiles, snap cubes, or even dice. Ask students to illustrate their findings with pictures and numbers. Give each partnership a chart to show what they find. Ask students to investigate the following questions:

- What products are possible?
- What's the greatest product?
- What's the least product?
- How could you organize what you've found to look for those patterns?
- What patterns do you notice in the products?

Discuss

Post students' charts around the room and give the class a few minutes to walk around and consider these questions:

- What different solutions did we find as a class?
- What interesting ways did we come up with to illustrate our findings?
- How could we organize our class findings to see patterns?
- What patterns do you see?

Discuss the different solutions students came up with, the ways they illustrated their findings, and the patterns students notice. Be sure to draw students' attention to effective ways of showing multiplication and ways of organizing solutions that help us see patterns. As a class, agree on a way to organize the findings to look for patterns and create a class chart with all the possible products that groups found.

As students look at these organized solutions, ask them what patterns they notice. Record these patterns on a second chart. Then name these as *conjectures,* or patterns that the class thinks might exist in other situations, too. Students can test these conjectures in the next round of exploration.

Explore

Partners investigate the question, How are these patterns the same or different if we start with a different number? Partners choose a sum other than 10 and explore whether the class's conjectures are always or only sometimes true. Continue to make manipulatives available for modeling this problem. Students illustrate their findings on charts and record their conclusions about the class conjectures, so others can see their evidence.

Discuss

Post students' charts and give the class a chance to walk around thinking about the big question: What patterns are always true? Discuss the patterns that exist for all numbers and any that are special to certain kinds of numbers. Return to the class chart of conjectures from the first round of investigation and ask, How did the class conjectures hold up to further investigation? How can we revise these conjectures based on our new findings?

Look-Fors

- **Are students understanding the constraints?** This puzzle can be challenging to understand because it involves a sum and a product. We encourage you to invest time during the launch to make the constraints of this task clear. Even still, some students may have trouble juggling the different ways that numbers are being used and may benefit from thinking of the puzzle in two parts, first the pairs of numbers that sum to 10 and then how to model multiplying those numbers. Bring students back to the language of the puzzle, which is stated in two separate sentences, to support students in breaking the puzzle into two parts.

- **How are students modeling multiplication?** Students may extend the models that they have used during the other lessons in this big idea, by using square tiles or dice. However, dice are a less convenient manipulative because they do not have 7s, 8s, 9s, 10s, or any larger value. That said, if students select dice, support them in thinking about when the dice could be used (say, for 6×4) and how they could build on this idea to model values for which the dice may be less useful. Students might create their own representations of 7, 8, 9, and 10 based on the dice arrangement and simply draw. Regardless of the specific manipulative students select, attend to how they interpret multiplication and represent the values as equal groups.

- **How are students thinking about looking for patterns?** Students very likely will not generate their solutions systematically. They might choose pairs of numbers as they come to mind, say $6 + 4$, then $2 + 8$, then $5 + 5$, and so on. When students record their models for multiplication, they will likely be in this same order, making it difficult to see patterns. After students have generated as many solutions as they can, ask questions about how these might be organized. For instance, they might be organized by the size of the product or by the values in the factor pairs, or by using some other system. Before students can organize their solutions, they'll need some support in considering what systems are possible and what they think will be the most revealing or useful. Draw on the thinking students start in their partnerships to fuel the whole-class discussion of how to organize the class's findings.

- **Are students investigating conjectures systematically?** During the second round of exploration, students should shift to investigating somewhat more systematically, building on their findings from the first round and the class's organized chart. Notice the ways students are becoming more organized to find pairs of factors, illustrate products, and look for evidence of the conjectures the class developed. If you see students continuing a random approach, you might refer them back to the more organized findings from the first round and ask how this could help them find all the possibilities or look for patterns. You may want to encourage students to choose a particular conjecture to look at closely, which could make their investigation more systematic. For instance, if students only want to investigate the conjecture that the largest product is the result of multiplying two numbers that are the same, they could examine only half of the combinations to gather evidence.

Reflect

What were the most surprising patterns you discovered in this investigation? Why were they surprising?

Two numbers add up to 10. What might you get if you multiply these numbers?

BIG IDEA 4

Tiling to Understand Area

In this big idea, we make connections between area and multiplication, enabling students to see multiplication visually. In our second big idea, students were invited to study perimeter, and in our third they considered equal groups. This next big idea progresses from these two, inviting students to engage creatively and visually. Geoboards are again used in this big idea, with the addition of square tiles that work really nicely with the geoboards. Mathematicians work every day on problems they do not know how to answer but tackle through working with innovation and creativity, which is part of the beauty of mathematics. In my own teaching, I have found it helpful to invite students to be investigators, asking their own questions and pursuing their own inquiries. When students have an investigator mindset, they often go beyond the problem assigned to them and morph or extend the problem to go deeper.

In the Visualize activity, students will create their own irregular shapes on a geoboard and work to find the area of the shape. This provides an opportunity for students to connect parts of unit squares, and we encourage you to help students visualize and learn to count pieces. We love that square tiles fit on the geoboard, and we encourage you to asks students to physically model the areas and then draw them on their own paper. Combining this with color coding as they write numerical expressions builds and strengthens important brain pathways. When students are struggling, I recommend that instead of helping them by structuring the work for them, you remind them that struggling helps their brains grow, and you assist them without taking away the cognitive challenge—for example, asking students to look

99

in different ways and to think creatively about ways to determine the area. I usually answer questions with another question that will help students think, or with the suggestion to draw what they are thinking. Encouraging students with growth-mindset messages and information about the positive effects of struggle for the brain and learning can be really rewarding.

Our Play activity brings in an image from the town of my first teaching job—London. Students will see that the letters of our alphabet can be formed in different ways using square tiles, and they are then invited to make their own alphabet using square tiles. We have added a constraint to encourage productive conversation and struggle, asking students which letters they can make if they have between 4 and 12 tiles to make each letter. Here students can explore, wonder, and later extend the activity as they build a deeper understanding of the ways square tiles add up to make area.

In our Investigate activity, we ask students to find different rectangles with an area of 24. We encourage students to make conjectures. Even though *conjecture* is a really important word in mathematics, students often do not know the word at all. I think of a conjecture as being an idea that you would like to test or try out, something you are not sure about. Mathematicians frequently make conjectures as they work. A conjecture is akin to a hypothesis in science. In my teaching, I share the word conjecture with students and name their different ideas with their names, saying this is Isabella's conjecture, for example. In this activity, we invite students to make group conjectures and then come together as a class to refine their work and make class conjectures. After this, they are invited to explore the conjectures. This activity concludes with a gallery walk where students walk around and study the work done by their peers. Encourage students to be curious about each other's ideas and to approach the mathematics they see with understanding. An important part of mathematical literacy is being able to read another piece of work with a critical eye, knowing that we can learn from others' mathematical thinking and writing.

Jo Boaler

Cover Up

Snapshot

Students use geoboards and square tiles to develop an understanding of area as covering with square units. Students make shapes on the geoboard to figure out, How big is this shape?

Connection to CCSS
3.MD.5, 3.MD.6
3.NF.1

Agenda

Activity	Time	Description/Prompt	Materials
Launch	5–10 min	Show students the irregular shape on the How Big Am I? sheet or on a geoboard. Ask students, How big is this shape? Focus attention on ways that describe the space, or area, rather than lengths.	Either the How Big Am I? sheet matching the size of geoboards you have, to display, or a geoboard and rubber band showing the same figure
Explore	20–30 min	Partners make shapes on geoboards and use square tiles to explore the question, How can we figure out how much space a shape takes up? Students record their shapes and strategies on Geoboard Sheets.	• Geoboard and rubber band, one per partnership • 1" square tiles, several per partnership • Geoboard Sheets, one or more sheets per partnership
Discuss	15 min	Partners share some of the shapes they have made and the strategies they have developed for finding how much space each one takes up. Discuss precision and how students can most accurately describe their findings. Name this attribute as area, or the number of square units needed to cover a shape.	• Geoboard, rubber band, and square tiles • Optional: chart paper, markers, and How Big Am I? sheet

(Continued)

Activity	Time	Description/Prompt	Materials
Extend	20 min	Choose two shapes students have made and whose area they have justified convincingly to the class. Ask students, What shapes can you make that have an area between these two shapes?	• Geoboard and rubber band, one per partnership • 1" square tiles, several per partnership • Geoboard Sheets, one or more sheets per partnership

To the Teacher

This lesson is designed to build the concept of area as covering with square units. Students do begin to count the area, but calculation is not the focus. Rather, the activity intends to support students in thinking about *what* it is that they are counting. Students will likely have had many experiences measuring linear distances, such as the side lengths of polygons, and they may be much more comfortable with thinking about shapes in relationship to the number of sides or the lengths of the sides. In this lesson, continue to bring students back to the notion of *space,* rather than how *long* the shape is. At the close of the lesson, tell students that the term we use for space is *area* and that it is measured in square units. At that point, students will have had the chance to cover their geoboards with square units, and the term will have meaning.

You'll notice that we have included two different Geoboard Sheets and two different images for launching the lesson. Geoboards come in two sizes: 5 × 5 and 7 × 7. It will be helpful if all of your students can use geoboards of the same size, though we don't think that one size is better than the other. We suggest you copy and share the sheets that match the size of the geoboards you have available.

Activity

Launch

Launch this activity by showing the figure on the geoboard shown on the How Big Am I? sheet. You can either display this sheet on a projector or re-create it on your own geoboard. Ask students, How big is this shape? Give students an opportunity to turn and talk to a partner about the question, What are some ways we can describe how big the shape is?

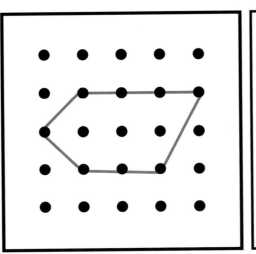

How Big Am I? image for 5 × 5 geoboards

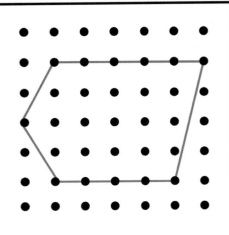

How Big Am I? image for 7 × 7 geoboards

Collect students' ideas. Students will likely come up with many different ways to describe how big the shape is, including the number of sides, how tall or wide it is, or estimates of the lengths of the sides. Draw students' attention to ways that describe the space (area) rather than just the sides (length or number), noting that if we describe how much space the shape takes up, that will most clearly describe its size. Tell students that today they're going to be exploring how we can describe how much space a shape takes up.

Explore

Provide partners with a geoboard and rubber band, 1" square tiles, and geoboard paper (matching the size of geoboards you have) for recording. Students explore the question, How can we figure out how much space a shape takes up? Students make any shape they want on the geoboard and develop ways to describe, using numbers and pictures, how much space the shape takes up. Students should record their thinking on geoboard paper so that others can see how they have figured out the space the each shape takes up.

Encourage partners to try lots of different shapes, including 3-sided, 4-sided, 5-sided, 6-sided shapes and so forth to see what happens. If students are only making shapes that include whole squares, ask them what they would do if the sides cut across squares.

As they explore, you might ask students, How can you put your shapes in order from smallest to largest? Students could choose to cut their geoboard paper into individual shapes so they can order them physically.

Discuss

Gather students together with their recording sheets and ask them to share some of the shapes they made and the strategies they developed for finding how much space a shape takes up. Have available a geoboard, rubber band, and square tiles so students can show their processes. Ask:

- What shapes did you make?
- How did you figure out how much space the shape takes up?
- How did you record your thinking?

Choose two shapes that groups made that students found to have similar areas (say, 12 and 14 squares). Ask the class, How can we be sure which one is bigger? Discuss the precision of the strategies students are using and how confident they are in the numbers of squares they have found for each shape. Some methods may turn out to be more accurate than others, as will some estimates. For instance, it may be more accurate to say that the area of a shape is "a little more than 10 squares, but less than 11 squares" than to say, "less than 11 squares" or "about 10 squares."

Tell students that what they have been measuring when they covered their shapes with squares is called *area*. Area is the number of square units needed to cover a shape completely. You may want to make a chart to display using this language and showing the figure from the How Big Am I? sheet. You might ask students to apply their strategies to the shape that the class started with and ask them to find its area, then label it on the chart to show how the class is thinking about area.

Extend

Choose two shapes that students have made and whose areas they have justified to the class. Ask students, Can you create a shape that has an area that is between these two? For instance, if you select shapes with areas of 12 and 17, students would try to make a shape with an area larger than 12 but smaller than 17. Again, provide students with geoboards, rubber bands, square tiles, and geoboard paper to explore.

Look-Fors

- **Are students focused on space?** Students may not have thought about measuring or counting space before, after years of focusing on linear measurements. Students may also have other ways of describing shapes using attributes such as number of sides or side lengths. A key move in this lesson is to focus students' thinking on space, in particular using square units as shown on the geoboard or the square tiles. If you notice students focused on other attributes, you may want to ask some probing questions about what those attributes describe, or restate what students have said. For instance, you might say, "I see you counting the edges, and you said that this side is four squares *long*. Instead of thinking about how long it is, how can we measure how much space the shape takes up?" You might also think about analogies that emphasize the space, such as, If these two shapes were cookies, how could you tell which one was bigger?

- **How are students dealing with partial squares?** Once students focus on space, counting up the whole squares is a matter of keeping track of which squares have been counted. But the partial squares represent a challenge. In cases where a square is cut in half, students may have the language and conceptual understanding to name the area of the partial square. In other cases, partial squares pose a bigger challenge. Students may be tempted to ignore partial squares. If you notice this, prompt students to question this assumption by asking, If you ignore these parts of the shape, are you really counting all the space? Students may count all partial squares as $\frac{1}{2}$, and you should question this use of the fraction, so that $\frac{1}{2}$ doesn't come to mean simply "part." You might ask, How do you know it is half? Or, What do you

mean by "half"? It may help students to shade in the whole squares on their geoboard sheets so they can better see the area that they have not yet described and to focus attention on asking, How much space *is* this? Another idea would be for them to color in part of the square in a color that is for the area of the shape and a different color for the area of the square that is not part of the shape area. This practice may support their understanding of pieces of the squares adding together to make one square.

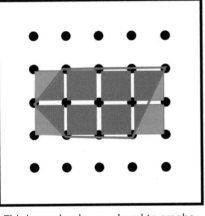

This image has been colored to emphasize the parts of a square that are part of the area and the parts that are not part of the area.

- **Have students made complex shapes?** Some students may be tempted to construct shapes that include a dozen sides and look like starbursts. These figures may have few or no whole squares in their area and will prove to be quite challenging to use early in the process of thinking about space. If students start with these shapes and get stumped, encourage them to record the shape on their geoboard paper to save it for later, and then to make a simpler shape to help them get started. They can either return to the complex shape after they have developed some strategies or present it to the class in the discussion as a challenge for all to help with.

- **How are students recording their thinking?** The Geoboard Sheets are intended as spaces to both capture and develop students' thinking. As students record what they have done with the square tiles or by counting with their fingers, these recording sheets can become places to help students track all the parts, show how they see partial squares coming together into wholes, or show how they might be using the spaces outside the shape to help them think about area. Encourage students to use the sheets to label the pieces and show how they come together into a measure of the space. Without these records, students will lose their thinking each time they move the rubber band. As you look at their records, one thing to attend to is whether students have recorded their shape accurately. Encourage students to check their shapes by counting the pegs or dots and make sure that the recording matches what they have made, so that the solutions on the geoboard and paper can reasonably match.

Reflect

What is area? Give one or more examples to show what area is.

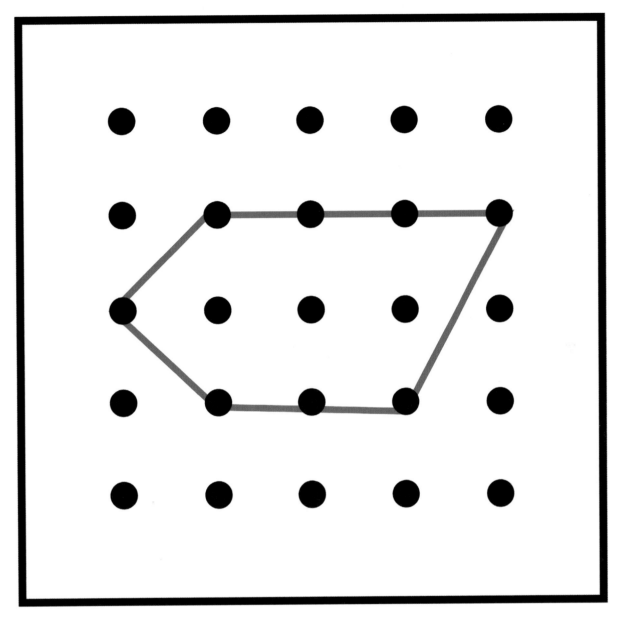

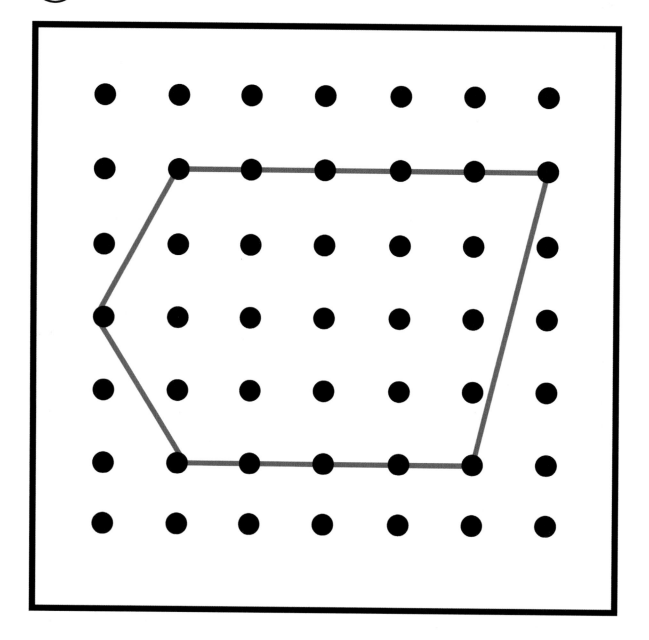

5 × 5 Geoboards

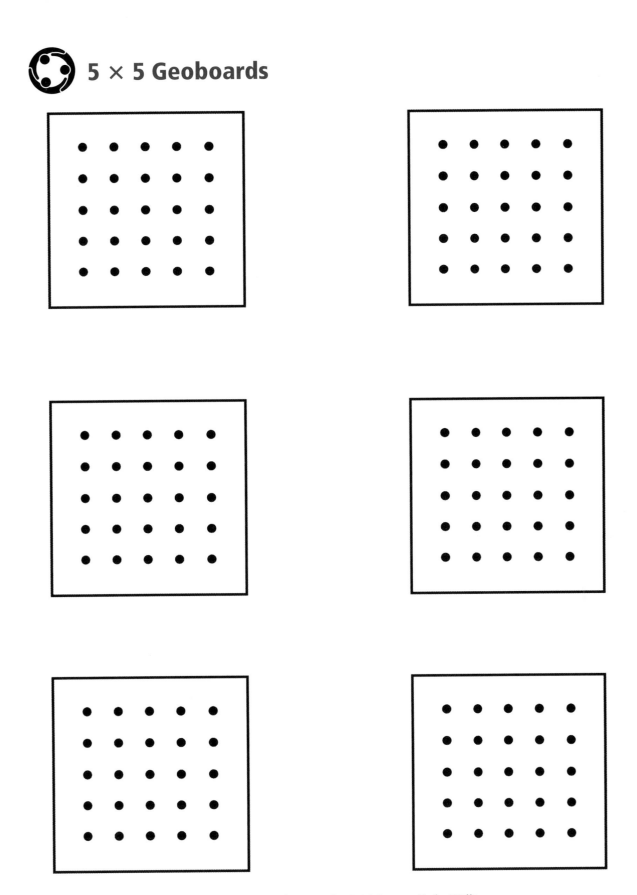

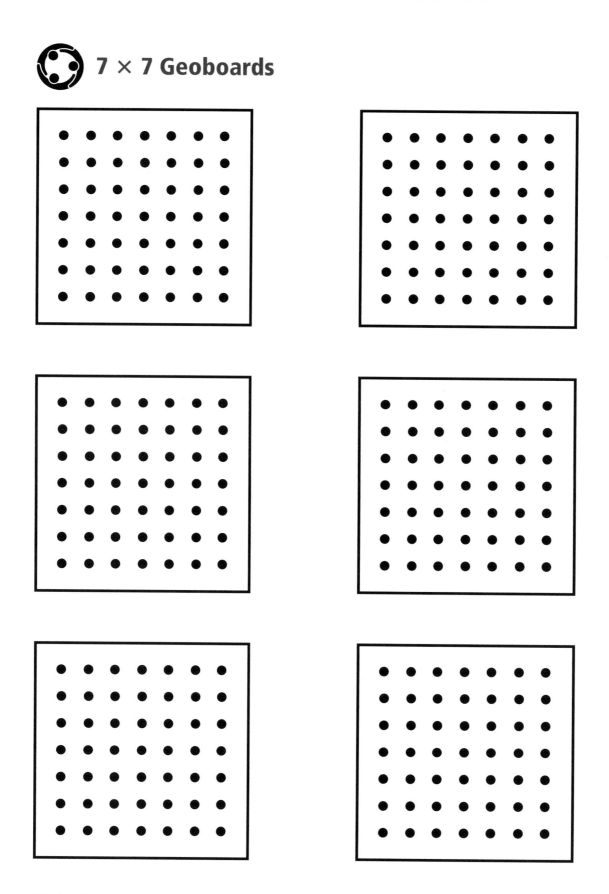

A Whole New Alphabet

Snapshot

Students play with area by building pixelated letters out of square units to see what letters could have an area of 4, 5, 6, and up to 12 square units.

Connection to CCSS
3.MD.5, 3.MD.6, 3.MD.7d

Agenda

Activity	Time	Description/Prompt	Materials
Launch	5–10 min	Show students the image on the One Way to Build a Z sheet and ask them what the area of this letter is. Tell students that there are lots of ways to build letters on a grid, and show the Train Station Sign image.	• One Way to Build a Z sheet, to display • Train Station Sign image, to display
Play	30 min	Partners use square tiles and grid or dot paper to explore the letters they can make with areas of 4, 5, 6, and up to 12 square units. Students record their findings and label the areas.	• Square tiles, at least 12 per partnership • Grid or dot paper (see appendix), multiple sheets per partnership
Discuss	15–20 min	Invite partners to share the letters they have created, starting with letters that have an area of 4 square units. Partners then record it on a Building Letters recording card and post it on a class display, organized so all letters with the same area are together. The class discusses what areas make the greatest number of letters, what letters can be made using different areas, and any letters that could not be made at all.	• Display space on a bulletin board or wall with labels for areas of 4 through 12 square units • Building Letters recording sheets, multiple sheets cut into quarters to serve as recording cards • Colors

Activity	Time	Description/Prompt	Materials
Extend	30+ min	Students create a full alphabet that shares the same height and width, and record the areas of each letter. Students explore what letters in their alphabet have the greatest and least area and what area is typical.	• Square tiles, for each partnership • Grid or dot paper (see appendix), multiple sheets per partnership

To the Teacher

In this activity, we take a different look at area by using whole square units to build letters, and describing their areas. As with the Visualize activity, we focus on the square unit and how figures can be built from squares. Students may ask if they can cut these units into parts to build their letters. We leave that decision to you. On the one hand, students have been working with partial units already and may be able to use $\frac{1}{2}$ squares effectively. This may provide an interesting challenge for the students who ask for it. On the other hand, signs that use squares to build letters, such as the train station sign shown in this activity or other pixelated alphabets, do not have $\frac{1}{2}$ units to work with. You could opt to extend this activity by allowing $\frac{1}{2}$ units and including new display spaces for $4\frac{1}{2}$, $5\frac{1}{2}$, $6\frac{1}{2}$ units, and so on. It might be interesting for students to explore what is possible when $\frac{1}{2}$ units are allowed and how that changes their findings.

Activity

Launch

Launch the activity by showing students the image on the One Way to Build a Z sheet. You might ask students if they have ever seen a letter built out of squares, like this one. Ask students, What is the area of the letter Z made this way?

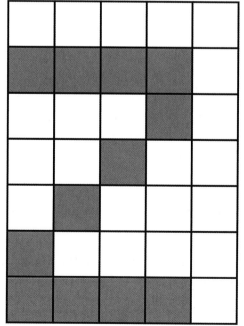

Give students a chance to turn and talk to a partner. Collect their ideas by inviting them to come up to the image and point to how they counted the area. Be sure that the class can agree on the area based on the number of squares it takes to cover the Z exactly.

Tell students there are lots of ways to make letters out of squares on a grid. Show students some examples of how people do this with letter signs, such as the Train Station Sign. You might ask students for examples of other places that they have seen these kinds of letters used, such as the "Open" sign at a convenience store or the pixelated letters used on computer games. Tell the class that in today's activity, they will be playing with ways to make letters with different areas on a grid.

Source: Image by Shutterstock.com/Duda Vasilii.

Play

Provide partners with square tiles and grid or dot paper (see appendix) for recording. Partners work together to figure out the following:

- What letters can you make with 4 tiles? 5 tiles? 6 tiles? And so on, up to 12 tiles.
- What letters can be made in different ways with different areas?
- What area can make the greatest number of letters?

As they play, students record all the letters they make and label each letter's area. Be sure to encourage students to use the language of *area* to describe the number of square tiles they use to build each letter.

Discuss

Create a class display space on a bulletin board or wall of the letters students made, organized by area, starting with 4 square units and building to 12 square units. Ask students to contribute the letters they made by asking them, What letters did you make with an area of 4 square units? Have students show on the document camera the letters they have made, and ask them to justify the area. When the class agrees that the letter does have this area, have the partners who created it draw it on a Building Letters recording card and post it under the appropriate area so that all solutions are represented.

Looking at the class display, discuss the following questions:

- What area can make the most letters?
- What letters can be made with many different areas?
- Were there any letters that you couldn't make? Why?
- Do you think we have found all the possible letters that can be made with these areas? Why or why not?

Extend

When an alphabet is built on a grid, letters typically share the same height, and many letters have the same width. Challenge students to find the smallest height and width that could be used to build all 26 letters of the alphabet. Ask students to create their alphabet and name the area needed for each letter. Ask students, What letter in your alphabet would have the greatest area? The least? What is a typical area? Provide students with square tiles and grid or dot paper (see appendix) for recording their alphabet.

Look-Fors

- **Are students building letters on a grid?** When students start with square tiles, they can assemble them in many ways, but a grid is locked into rows and columns. Some students may struggle to use the square tiles in this way and may find it physically easier to simply use grid or dot paper (see appendix). Others may prefer to start with a fixed number of tiles and be able to move them around. If you notice that students are not aligning their tiles in rows and columns, you can draw students' attention to the ways that their use of the tiles does or does not match the way the grid is set up. Providing copies of 1" grid paper (see appendix) to use as a structure for placing the square tiles may also support students in thinking in rows and columns.

- **Are students using the vocabulary of area?** Encourage students to use the language of area as they describe the letters they have built. Some students may talk about "using five squares" to build a letter. Revoice these expressions as, "So you built a letter with an area of 5 square units?" Be sure that you are also using this language when you ask students what area they are working on.

Reflect

If you were to make the digits 0–9 on a grid, which digit do you think would have the greatest area? The least? Why?

One Way to Build a Z

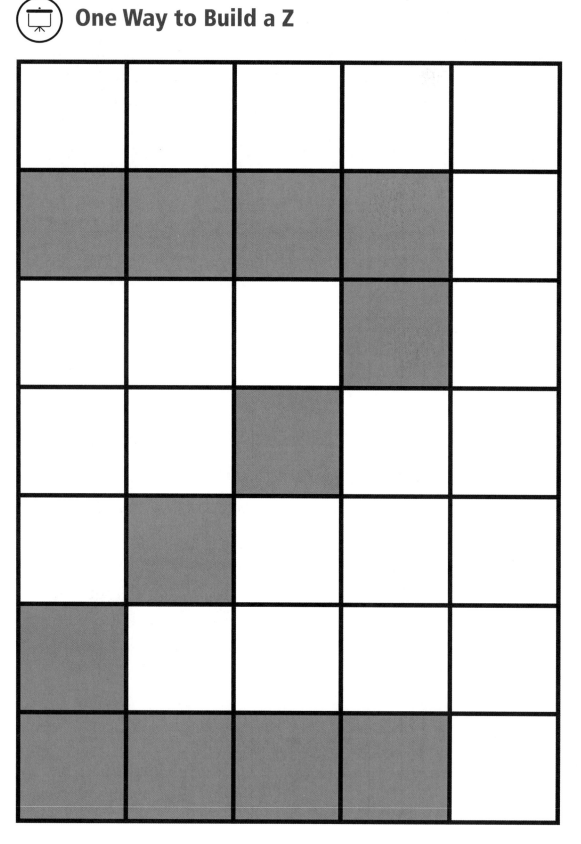

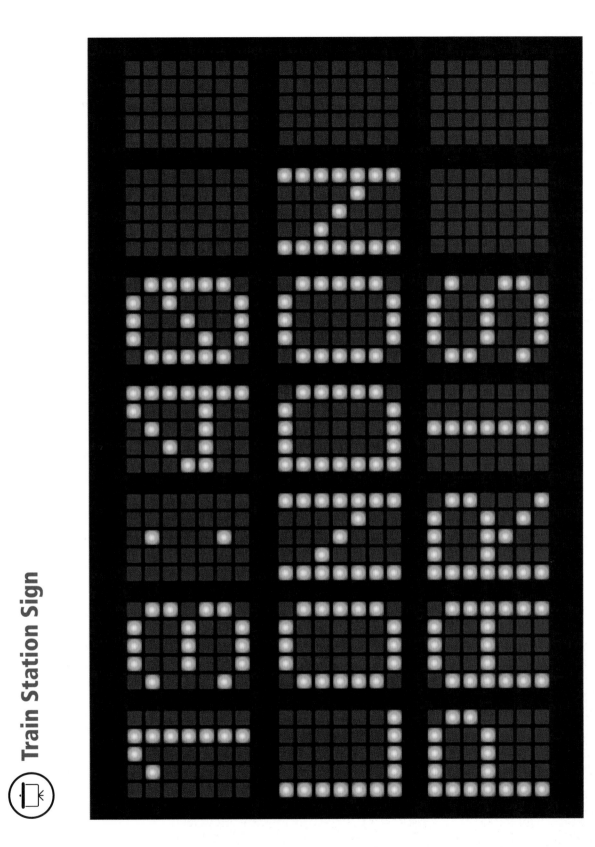

Mindset Mathematics, Grade 3, copyright © 2018 by Jo Boaler, Jen Munson, Cathy Williams.
Reproduced by permission of John Wiley & Sons, Inc. *Source:* Image by Shutterstock.com/Duda Vasilii.

Building Letters

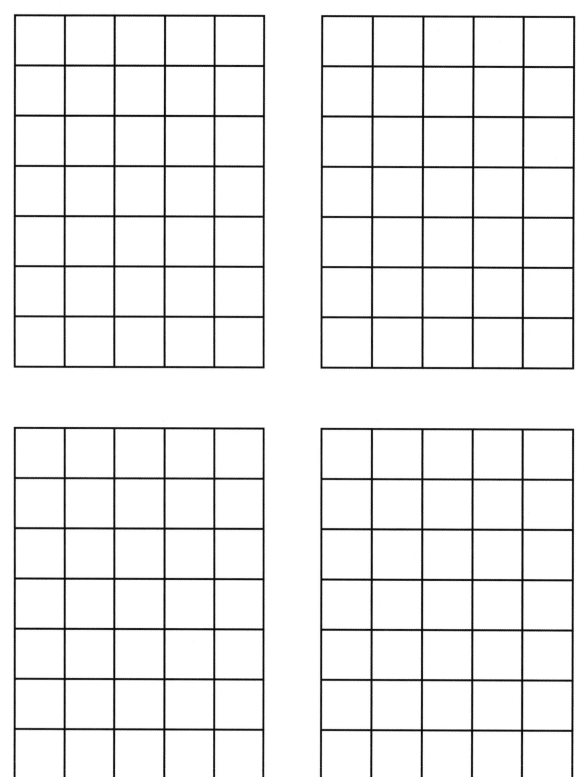

Mindset Mathematics, Grade 3, copyright © 2018 by Jo Boaler, Jen Munson, Cathy Williams.
Reproduced by permission of John Wiley & Sons, Inc.

Sharing an Area

Snapshot

Students create rectangles with the same area and look for patterns, opening the door to connecting area and multiplication.

Connection to CCSS
3.MD.5, 3.MD.6, 3.MD.7a

Agenda

Activity	Time	Description/Prompt	Materials
Launch	5 min	Show students four square tiles and ask, What rectangles can we make with an area of 4 square units? Invite students to make rectangles and discuss whether rotating the rectangle makes a different rectangle.	Four square tiles
Explore	20 min	Partners make as many rectangles as they can with an area of 24 square units, using square tiles and dot or grid paper. They record and label all the rectangles they make.	• Square tiles, 24 per partnership • Grid or dot paper (see appendix), multiple sheets per partnership
Discuss	15 min	Students share the rectangles they made with an area of 24 square units, and the class discusses how they know the rectangles' areas. The class looks for patterns in rectangles with the same area and makes conjectures.	• Chart and markers • Optional: grid or dot paper (see appendix)

Activity	Time	Description/Prompt	Materials
Explore	20–30 min	Partners test the class's conjectures about rectangles with the same area by choosing a new area and making rectangles with that area. Partners create a chart of their findings and any evidence that supports or conflicts with the class's conjectures.	• Chart and markers, for each partnership • Make available: dot and grid paper (see appendix), scissors, tape, and square tiles
Discuss	20 min	Post partners' charts and do a gallery walk, looking for what evidence the class agrees on and what conflicting evidence the class found. Discuss the evidence for the conjectures and revise the class's chart. Discuss any new patterns or questions that emerge.	Chart and markers

To the Teacher

This investigation is intended to open the door to Big Idea 5, Seeing Multiplication as Area. We begin with our first focused look at the area of rectangles, and students generate rectangles with a given area. Then the class develops some ways to name or label these rectangles by focusing on their side lengths. Although we typically think of naming rectangles using multiplication, such as 3 × 8 and saying "3 by 8," this may not be the language students use at the beginning. Accept the many variations that students may come up with, such as "3 wide and 8 long," and record them all together. The activity is not meant to be specifically about multiplication, but simply to begin to look at the patterns that emerge from area so that in future work the connection between multiplication and area will make sense.

As part of this investigation, students may go beyond thinking in whole units and rotate their rectangles on the grid like the one shown here.

This is difficult area work, and although it is not the focus of this activity, students can certainly choose to pursue these kinds of rectangles in addition to those positioned on the grid lines.

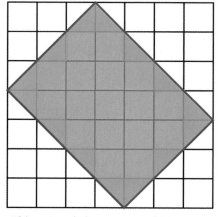

This rectangle has an area of 24 square units: 17 red tiles and 14 green half tiles.

These rotated, or oblique, rectangles pose two particular challenges. First, students will need to find strategies for proving the area by accurately piecing together partial squares. Second, the dimensions are not clear, and they cannot be labeled as 3×4 or any other pair of whole numbers. If students explore these rectangles, they will need to create a different way to label them, and the patterns they notice in the rectangles that are on grid lines may not fit with these oblique rectangles. We describe these challenges not to discourage you and students from exploring these rectangles but rather to prepare you for the conversations that might emerge when students take this intellectual risk.

Activity

Launch

Launch this activity by reminding students of the work they did with creating letters with a particular area in the Play activity. Tell students that today they are going to focus on making rectangles with a particular area. Show students four square tiles and ask, What rectangles can we make with an area of 4 square units? Invite students to come up to the document camera to show different ways they could arrange the tiles into a rectangle with an area of 4 square units. Students will likely create a square and a long rectangle. If students orient this long rectangle vertically or horizontally, be sure to note that these can be seen as different or the same, depending on the circumstance. For instance, if it were a pencil, it would simply be turned but not changed. But if it were a building, a long low building is different from a tall skinny one. Tell students that today they will be making rectangles that all have the same area and that for this activity, turning the rectangle will make a new solution.

Explore

Provide partners with dot or grid paper (see appendix) and square tiles. Students investigate the following questions:

- What rectangles can we make with an area of 24 square units?
- How can we name those rectangles so that we can compare and discuss them?
- Can we find all the possibilities?

Students record on their dot or grid paper (see appendix) all of their solutions, with labels. Some students may want to start with tiles and build each rectangle before recording it. But if students seem ready, they can try creating rectangles directly on the grid or dot paper. This opens up the possibility of making rectangles that are oblique, or set on an angle to the grid lines. Doing so makes it more challenging to prove the area and to use the square tiles, but if students try this, encourage them to puzzle out the area. They might want to cut the shapes out or do other things to prove the area.

Discuss

Gather students together and discuss the following questions:

- What shapes did you make that have an area of 24 square units? (Record these on a chart or sheet of grid or dot paper [see appendix] for everyone to see.)
- How do you know what the area is? (This is particularly important for oblique rectangles.)
- How do we know whether we have found all the possibilities?
- How did we label the rectangles? (Encourage ways that describe the side lengths, as this is what distinguishes different rectangles. This works well for rectangles on the grid lines, rather than the oblique rectangles.)
- What patterns do you see?

Using what the class has noticed, make some conjectures about rectangles with the same area. This involves suggesting that one or more of the patterns in these rectangles might be true for all rectangles with the same area. For instance, students might conjecture that you can always turn a rectangle to get a new rectangle so that a 2-unit by 12-unit rectangle can become a 12-unit by 2-unit rectangle. Record these conjectures on a class chart.

Explore

Partners explore one or more of the conjectures the class has made by choosing a different area and making rectangles with that area. Note that the area that partners choose makes a difference for what students find. Encourage students to choose an area under 40 square units to keep it manageable. Students try to answer the following questions:

- How do you find all the possible rectangles with a chosen area?
- What patterns do you notice in rectangles with the same area?

- Are these patterns the same as or different from those the class found for rectangles with an area of 24 square units?
- What evidence did you find to support the class's conjectures?
- What evidence did you find that conflicts with the class's conjectures?

Partners create a display of the area they explored, the rectangles they found, and the evidence they gathered about the class's conjectures. Provide students with charts, markers, grid or dot paper (see appendix), square tiles, scissors, and tape to investigate and to create their display.

Discuss

Post students' charts around the classroom. Invite students to do a gallery walk by walking around the room to examine the charts others have made and the evidence they have collected. Ask students, What do we seem to agree on? What conflicting evidence did we find?

As a class, discuss the following questions:

- What evidence did we find regarding our class conjectures? What support did we find?
- What ideas need revision?
- What other evidence might we need to gather?
- What new patterns do you notice?
- What new questions do you have?

Make revisions to the class conjectures chart based on what the class has found, confirming, crossing out, or revising the conjectures. In this discussion, students may begin to notice that some areas have more rectangles than others, particularly if students focus on making rectangles on the grid lines of the grid paper. Some may notice that there is a connection to multiplication, that a 3-unit by 4-unit rectangle has 3×4 square units in its area. Whatever students notice can be recorded on a chart and can serve to fuel thinking about the next big idea in this book, Seeing Multiplication as Area.

Look-Fors

- **Are students thinking systematically?** As students begin exploration of rectangles with the same area, they may work through trial and error, just assembling tiles until they find a rectangle and then shuffling them to try again.

Encourage students to use what they have found to generate new rectangles by asking them, How could you change this rectangle to make a new one? For instance, students might fold a long rectangle in half, turning a 1×24 into a 2×12 rectangle. Alternatively, students may get stuck assuming that they can select one side length and find a way to make it work. For instance, students may decide that they want one side to be 5 units long and then get stuck trying again and again to make this work. You might ask, Why do you think it's so hard to make 5 units work?

- **Are students noticing the connection to multiplication or equal groups?** Encourage any connections students make to seeing rows or columns as equal groups. For instance, students might notice that a rectangle that is 3 units by 8 units is like 3 groups of 8 squares or 8 groups of 3 squares. If you record the labels for the rectangles as "3 by 8" or "3×8," students may ask if that means multiplication. You can ask them to explore that question themselves: Are rectangles like multiplication? How?

- **How are students organizing their evidence?** In the second part of this investigation, students will be looking for evidence that supports or contradicts the conjectures the class has come up with. They will need to be systematic about looking for and sharing their evidence so that they can convince others. This includes finding all the rectangles for the area they chose, presenting them with labels, and recording how they compare to what the class found in the first part of the investigation.

- **Have students chosen an area with few rectangles?** Students who choose a prime number for the area may get frustrated trying to find multiple solutions. Be sure to encourage them to search, but ask probing questions that help them think about whether they may have found all the possible rectangles. For instance, you might ask, What have you tried? What else can you try? Do you think you might have found all the rectangles? Why? How can you be sure? If students have exhausted the rectangles possible, focus them on how what they found supports or conflicts with the class conjectures. They may want to try another area to gather additional evidence.

Reflect

What did you notice in the rectangles today that surprised you? What are you wondering now?

Seeing Multiplication as Area

In this big idea, we think about change, with such questions as, How does area change when perimeter changes? We also ask students to think about "near-squares," which, as their name suggests, are rectangles that are nearly squares. Both of these activities will help students see mathematics as a flexible subject—instead of as a fixed list of rules and methods. When I teach students, I often share with them the value of a particular mathematical practice of taking a smaller case. Instead of investigating with really big numbers, for example, they might try some smaller numbers first. When I have suggested this to different schoolchildren in the past, many have been resistant, thinking that changing the question is somehow cheating and is not what you do in math. This tells me that they have a fixed view of math and do not see it as something they need to act on and play with in order to make progress. It is helpful to always help students see mathematics as something that is flexible and changeable.

In the introduction to the book, I wrote about the importance of students approaching mathematics conceptually so that they can compress concepts in their brains. Compression is a central process in mathematics learning. In this big idea, we offer many opportunities for students to think conceptually and flexibly about area and perimeter. Students will be invited to focus on connecting multiplication and area in visual ways and to find area by counting square units inside rectangles.

In our Visualize activity, we bring in one of my favorite manipulatives: Cuisenaire rods. We ask students to use rods as the perimeter of rectangles and think about the different ways the rods can be placed to form a rectangle. Students can then explore patterns and wonder about the same rods defining different areas. Why aren't the areas the same when you use the same rods to build different rectangles?

The Play activity provides students with the chance to use the multiplication table for pattern-seeking. We ask questions such as, Why are near-squares just one unit away from the square number and always on a diagonal? Students will work to make sense of the patterns while making squares and near-squares out of tiles. We ask students to draw what they have constructed and think about how they see the tiles moving as they consider square and near-square shapes.

In our Investigate activity, students are asked to explore the different rectangles they can make with a set number of square tiles. This will help them think about the same ideas in different ways. Our goal is to support students in understanding the difference between area and perimeter. We do not focus on formulas but on understanding conceptually the connections between a linear measure like perimeter and an area measure. Students will again be invited to make conjectures as they create and study patterns and investigate whether rectangles with a fixed area have the same perimeter.

Jo Boaler

Rods Around

Snapshot

Students begin to connect area with multiplication by exploring the areas of different rectangles formed using the same Cuisenaire rods.

> Connection to CCSS
> 3.MD.5, 3.MD.6, 3.MD.7
> 3.OA.1

Agenda

Activity	Time	Description/Prompt	Materials
Launch	10 min	Ask students to use two brown and two purple Cuisenaire rods to make rectangles. Make as many different rectangles as possible and name these for the students who first created them.	Six brown and six purple Cuisenaire rods
Explore	25–30 min	Partners use Cuisenaire rods to explore the question, Are the areas of the rectangles inside the rods the same? Why or why not? Students develop ways of recording their findings to look for patterns.	• Cuisenaire rods set, one per partnership • Centimeter grid paper (see appendix), multiple sheets per partnership
Discuss	15+ min	Discuss the central question of this activity by collecting some of the class's findings. Record the rods used, rectangles made, and areas on a chart. Focus on the role of the side lengths in finding the area, and name that the area of a rectangle can be found by multiplying the side lengths that represent the height and width.	Chart and markers

In this activity, we begin to think about the area of rectangles by making different rectangles using pieces of the same length. We use Cuisenaire rods to explore building frames around rectangles. It is critical to note that for this activity, we focus on the rectangles that can be seen inside the rods—the window that is created, not the frame. You will need to draw students' attention to this inner rectangle so that everyone is talking about the same shape.

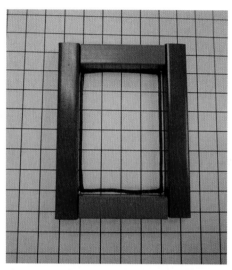

This is one of the inner rectangles possible when using two brown and two purple rods.

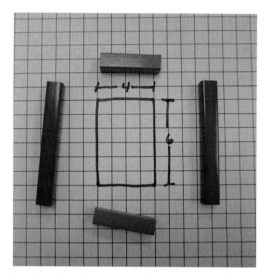

The 4 × 6 cm inner rectangle has an area of 24 sq cm.

Cuisenaire rods are each a whole number of centimeters long, with rods starting at 1cm, growing incrementally through 10 cm. If the rods are laid on top of centimeter grid paper (see appendix), as we have suggested here, the window created by the rods can be positioned so that a clear rectangle can be seen inside the rods. This rectangle will have whole-number side lengths. Students can draw the rectangle, count the side lengths, and count the area.

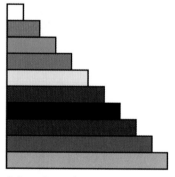

Cuisenaire rods

Students should, for each combination of two different pairs of rods, be able to make three rectangles. One will be longer and skinnier, with the shorter rod length on the outside; one will be closer to a square, with the longer rod length on the outside. The final rectangle arranges the rods in a spiral and will likely be the last kind of rectangle found. Be sure students find all three arrangements before sending them off to explore the question of the day: Are the areas of the rectangles inside the rods the same? Why or why not? It stands to reason that these rectangles might all have the same area, since they were made from the same pieces, but perimeter and area are different attributes. This activity may open conversation about this relationship as students explore why the areas are different.

Activity

Launch

Launch the activity by showing two brown and two purple Cuisenaire rods on the document camera. Ask students, What rectangles can we make with these Cuisenaire rods? Invite students to come up and make different rectangles. It will be useful to have extra rods so that the different rectangles can be seen side by side. Each rectangle, however, should use two brown and two purple rods. As students develop different ways to make rectangles, name them by the student who first suggested it (Jo's way, Cathy's way, and Jen's way, for example). The three different possible rectangles are shown here.

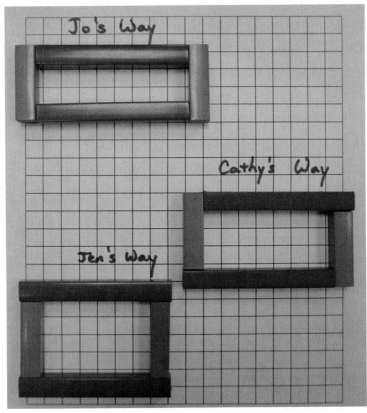

The three different ways you can make different rectangles with two brown and two purple Cuisenaire rods

Pose the question for today: Are the areas of the rectangles inside the rods the same? Why or why not? Ask students to turn and talk, then collect their predictions and reasoning.

Explore

Partners choose two pairs of Cuisenaire rods to use to try to answer the question, Are the areas of the rectangles made with the same Cuisenaire rods the same? Why or why not? Students use centimeter grid paper (see appendix) to record the rectangles they make and their areas, to look for patterns. Note that the centimeter grid paper should align with the Cuisenaire rods so that rectangles with whole-number side lengths are created.

Partners can repeat this exploration with different pairs of rods, though we recommend not using the white (1 cm) and red (2 cm) rods, which are too small. Ask students to develop a way of recording their findings, perhaps in a table, to help them find patterns across the different rods they try.

Discuss

As a class, discuss the central question: Are the areas of the rectangles made by the same Cuisenaire rods the same? Why or why not?

Collect some examples from partnerships to serve as shared data. Ask students to justify the areas they have found by showing the strategies they have developed. Record on a chart the rods students used, the rectangles they made, and the areas they found. Once the class agrees that they do not have the same area, press students to discuss why. Focus attention on the side lengths, if they come up in the discussion of why the areas are different. Ask students what patterns they notice when looking at the side lengths and areas. Students may notice that the areas are the result of multiplying the side lengths; if they do notice the connection, be sure to name this clearly for students and record it on your chart.

Look-Fors

- **Are students focusing on the rectangles inside the rods?** As noted earlier, students will need some support in focusing on the rectangle inside the border formed by the Cuisenaire rods, rather than on the rectangle formed by the outside edges of the rods. As you circulate through the classroom, pay attention to how students are marking off the rectangle or where they are counting the squares. If you see students tracing the outside edge of the rods or lifting the rods up to count squares underneath, intervene to clarify which rectangle the class is focusing on today.

- **How are students finding the areas of their rectangles?** Students will likely use a variety of strategies on a trajectory to connecting area to multiplication, two new concepts in third grade. Students may simply count the squares one by one. Students may develop more efficient counting strategies, such as skip counting. They may use repeated addition, grouping the squares by rows or columns, whichever is easiest to add. They may think in "groups of" or "rows of" squares. They may even decompose the rectangle into pieces they know, such as cutting a 3×6 rectangle into two 3×3 squares, knowing that each is like a tic-tac-toe board and has 9 squares. Encourage students to use whatever strategies make sense to them, and expose students to the strategies that others use to help them grow their thinking.

- **Are students making connections between multiplication, equal groups, and area?** In previous big ideas, we have explored the concept of equal groups and their relationship to multiplication, and the concept of area as square units covering a space. Focusing on rectangles creates opportunities for students to see the rows and columns of square units on grid paper as both area and equal groups. Look for signs that students are making connections between area and multiplication, such as using skip counting or repeated addition. Build on students' language, such as describing the area as "3 rows of 6." You might note that "3 rows of 6" is like "three 6s" or "6 and 6 and 6." You might also ask students, "So how can we find out how much 3 groups of 6 is?" Help students see the connections between all these ways of describing and thinking about area, equal groups, and multiplication.

Reflect

What are some different ways you can find the area of a rectangle?

Squares and Near-Squares

Snapshot

Students play with the areas of squares and *near-squares*, or rectangles that are one unit shorter and one unit longer than squares, to find a relationship. Students connect this relationship to multiplication in an extension that involves the multiplication table.

Connection to CCSS
3.MD.5, 3.MD.6, 3.MD.7
3.OA.9

Agenda

Activity	Time	Description/Prompt	Materials
Launch	5–10 min	Show students a 4 × 4 square and ask them what they know about its area. Then ask what would happen to the area if one side got a little shorter but the other got a little longer. Show students a 3 × 5 rectangle, or *near-square*, and ask them to predict whether its area is the same as, smaller than, or larger than the 4 × 4 square.	Square and Near-Square Sheet, to display
Play	20–30 min	Partners play with the relationship between the areas of squares and near-squares by building, drawing, and finding their areas. Students record their findings on a table to help them look for patterns.	• Square tiles and grid paper (see appendix), for each partnership • Square and Near-Square Table, one per partnership

Activity	Time	Description/Prompt	Materials
Discuss	15+ min	Collect students' findings on a class chart that mirrors students' recording sheet. Ask the class, What patterns do you see? What is the relationship between the areas of squares and near-squares? How can we use tiles or drawing to see that relationship?	Chart and markers
Extend	25+ min	Provide students with a multiplication table and ask them, How can we see the relationship between squares and near-squares on the multiplication table? Students color-code or mark up the table to see the relationship and discuss how it connects to their previous work.	Multiplication Table sheet, one or more per partnership

To the Teacher

This activity gives students lots of opportunities to make rectangles, count the side lengths, and find area in an effort to identify larger patterns and relationships. As you circulate through the classroom, be sure to take note of the strategies students are using and how they are developing as students work. Students will want to find patterns that make counting the area easier, moving from counting each individual tile to thinking in groups with repeated addition or skip counting, and eventually moving toward multiplicative thinking.

The relationship this activity explores is one that is rarely discussed in schools. We begin by looking at a 4×4 square, whose area is 16 square units, or 4 rows of 4. If you make one side just one unit shorter and the other side one unit longer, you get a 3×5 rectangle, whose area is 15 square units, or 3 rows of 5 (see the figure that follows). You'll notice that this area is very close, but not equal, to the area of the square. In fact, the area of a near-square will always be one square unit smaller. Why? We encourage you to try this with tiles and drawings yourself or with colleagues. It is a pattern more easily understood visually than numerically. Notice what happens when you move the tiles from the top of the square to the side. Why is the area one less?

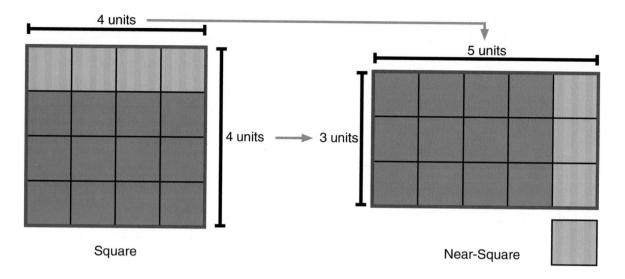

4 units

4 units → 3 units

5 units

Square

Near-Square

The extension activity offers an interesting way of introducing the multiplication table. Often this tool is misused for rote memorization, but here we incorporate it for its power as a set of patterns. We encourage students to use color coding to make clear connections between all that they have constructed with their hands and the patterns in the table. Afterward you may choose to display the colorful patterns your students have discovered. By introducing the multiplication table in this way, it can become a site of inquiry and inspire students to wonder about the many patterns it contains.

X	1	2	3	4	5	6	7	8	9	10	11	12
1	1	2	3	4	5	6	7	8	9	10	11	12
2	2	4	6	8	10	12	14	16	18	20	22	24
3	3	6	9	12	15	18	21	24	27	30	33	36
4	4	8	12	16	20	24	28	32	36	40	44	48
5	5	10	15	20	25	30	35	40	45	50	55	60
6	6	12	18	24	30	36	42	48	54	60	66	72
7	7	14	21	28	35	42	49	56	63	70	77	84
8	8	16	24	32	40	48	56	64	72	80	88	96
9	9	18	27	36	45	54	63	72	81	90	99	108
10	10	20	30	40	50	60	70	80	90	100	110	120
11	11	22	33	44	55	66	77	88	99	110	121	132
12	12	24	36	48	60	72	84	96	108	120	132	144

Activity

Launch

Launch the activity by showing students a 4 × 4 square on the document camera. You can draw and label this square on grid paper (see appendix), or display the one shown on the Square and Near-Square Sheet. If you use the sheet, cover the near-square to focus students on the square. Ask students, What do we know about the area of this square? Give students a chance to turn and talk to a partner, and then take some student ideas. Students will have different ways of explaining what the area of the square is and how they know.

Ask students, What happens to the area if we make one side longer, but we make the other side shorter? Show students a 3 × 5 rectangle, either by drawing a new rectangle next to the square or by revealing the rectangle on the Square and Near-Square Sheet. Make sure students see that one side has been made one unit shorter and the other side has been made one unit longer. Tell students we're going to call this a *near-square*. Then give students a moment to make a prediction: Did the area change? Do you think the area of the near-square is the same as, smaller than, or larger than the area of the square? Why? Give students a moment to turn and talk to a partner about their predictions and the reasoning behind them.

Play

Partners play with the relationship between the area of a square and that of a near-square: Is the area of the near-square the same as, smaller than, or larger than the area of the square? Why? Provide students with square tiles, grid paper (see appendix), and a Square and Near-Square Table to explore and record. Encourage students to make several squares and their near-squares to explore these questions:

- What patterns do you notice?
- What is the relationship between the area of a square and the area of a near-square?
- How can you see that relationship with tiles or drawings?

Discuss

Create a table on chart paper that mirrors the Square and Near-Square Table students have been using. Invite partners to share their findings of the areas of different square and near-square pairs. With this chart as a class reference, discuss the following questions:

- What patterns do you notice?
- What is the relationship between the area of a square and the area of a near-square?
- Will that relationship always be the same? Why or why not?
- How can we use tiles or pictures to help us see what is happening with the areas of these rectangles as we change the side lengths?

Invite students to show their own drawings or to use square tiles to show what is happening when a square is changed to a near-square so that the class can see the relationship between the areas in different ways, connecting the table to tiles to drawings.

If students have not yet noticed the connection between multiplication and area, focus the class's discussion on the two pairs of columns where side lengths and area are shown side by side. You might ask the class, What is the relationship between the side lengths and the area?

Extend

Give students a copy of the Multiplication Table sheet. If students have never seen a multiplication table, you may need to provide some opportunity for them to notice its structure and what it shows. Ask, How do the patterns of squares and near-squares show up on the multiplication table? Ask students to color-code or mark up the multiplication table to show their findings. Ask, How does this change your understanding about what is going on? How does it connect to what the class found when building the squares and near-squares? What new questions do you have?

Look-Fors

- **How are students finding the areas of the rectangles?** Just as in the previous lesson, it is useful to observe how students find areas, knowing that these strategies will develop over time. At this point, students may be shifting away from counting the tiles or squares by 1s, and toward thinking about skip counting, repeated addition, decomposing the rectangle into smaller pieces, or multiplication. Often as students try new strategies, you may see them checking their results using a strategy, such as counting, that they feel more confident about. Encourage this sense making; it creates connections between strategies and mathematical ideas such as counting, addition, equal groups, and multiplication.

- **Where are students seeing the relationship between the areas of squares and near-squares?** Some students may see the relationship in the table first, when the examples begin to accumulate and students see the numbers. Other students might see the relationship by building squares with tiles and then physically shifting them to make a near-square, always having one tile left over. Others may see this relationship in drawings, by putting the two figures side by side, or even layering them on grid paper to better see the change. When talking with students about their work, you'll want to draw connections between the squares and near-squares, and connections between these different ways of seeing their relationship.

- **How are students making sense out of the multiplication table?** If students have never seen the multiplication table, we encourage you to allow them some time just to look at it and make sense of it. It is important to keep in mind how different this table looks from most of the tools we use in mathematics, and it contains many, many relationships. Ask students what the table shows and what it means. Give them time to wonder about it and make observations. Be sure that they notice the relationship between the value at the intersection of the points on the axes as the area of a rectangle with those side lengths, or as the product of those two factors. Understanding how to read the table through some inquiry should come before trying to connect the table to the patterns students have already explored. Once students are ready to move on to this work, look for how they are marking their findings on the multiplication table. You may want to encourage students to start by simply finding on the table the squares and near-squares they build themselves.

Reflect

How are area and multiplication related? Draw a picture to show your thinking.

Square and Near-Square Sheet

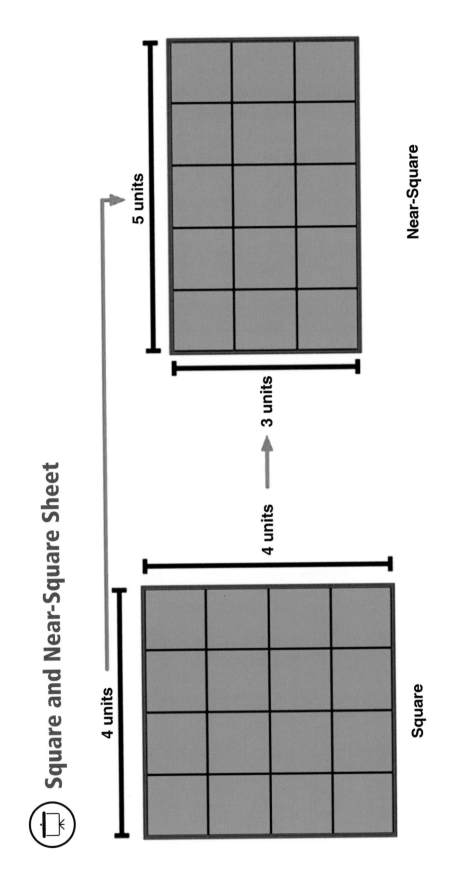

Near-Square

5 units

3 units

4 units

4 units

Square

Square and Near-Square Table

Square Length and Width	Square Area	Near-Square Length and Width	Near-Square Area

Multiplication Table

X	1	2	3	4	5	6	7	8	9	10	11	12
1	1	2	3	4	5	6	7	8	9	10	11	12
2	2	4	6	8	10	12	14	16	18	20	22	24
3	3	6	9	12	15	18	21	24	27	30	33	36
4	4	8	12	16	20	24	28	32	36	40	44	48
5	5	10	15	20	25	30	35	40	45	50	55	60
6	6	12	18	24	30	36	42	48	54	60	66	72
7	7	14	21	28	35	42	49	56	63	70	77	84
8	8	16	24	32	40	48	56	64	72	80	88	96
9	9	18	27	36	45	54	63	72	81	90	99	108
10	10	20	30	40	50	60	70	80	90	100	110	120
11	11	22	33	44	55	66	77	88	99	110	121	132
12	12	24	36	48	60	72	84	96	108	120	132	144

Connecting Area and Perimeter

Snapshot

The class investigates the relationship between area and perimeter by exploring the perimeters of rectangles that have the same area. The class creates a display they can use to detect patterns, make conjectures, and test their ideas.

> Connection to CCSS
> 3.MD.5, 3.MD.6, 3.MD.7
> 3.MD.8

Agenda

Activity	Time	Description/Prompt	Materials
Launch	5–10 min	Ask students to create different rectangles with 12 square tiles. Ask the class, Do you think all these rectangles, made with the same area, have the same perimeter? Students make predictions with reasons.	Square tiles, to display
Explore	20 min	Partners choose an area to explore, and construct several rectangles with that area. Students find the perimeter of each rectangle and then construct models on 1" grid paper, labeling each with its perimeter. Partners post their rectangles on the class display, in order from the shortest to the longest perimeter with the same area.	• Square tiles and grid paper (see appendix), for each partnership • 1" grid paper (see appendix), scissor, and tape, for making rectangles to display • Display space with labels for area, shortest perimeter, and longest perimeter
Discuss	15 min	After a few rows of data have been added to the class display, discuss the patterns students are beginning to notice. Make and record some class conjectures. Students may note potential errors and highlight these as places for further investigation.	• Class display of rectangles • Chart and markers

Activity	Time	Description/Prompt	Materials
Explore	25–30 min	Partners return to the investigation to add more data to the class display, test the class's conjectures, determine if any potential error in the class display needs to be corrected, and look for new patterns.	• Square tiles and grid paper (see appendix), for each partnership • 1" grid paper (see appendix), scissor, and tape, for making rectangles to display • Display space with labels for area, shortest perimeter, and longest perimeter
Discuss	15+ min	Discuss the patterns students notice in the class display, the evidence students have collected, and any revisions they want to make to the conjectures based on this evidence. Discuss the relationship between area and perimeter that they can see in the data.	• Class display of rectangles • Conjectures chart and markers

To the Teacher

Up to this point, we have been careful to introduce perimeter and area at different times and to build conceptual understanding of each. Perimeter is the distance around an object or shape, and we hope students can call up a physical memory of encircling an object with string whenever they think about perimeter. Area is the number of square units needed to cover a shape or surface, and we hope that students have a physical memory of tiling geoboards and constructing rectangles with square tiles. In this investigation, we explore the relationship between perimeter and area as two attributes of shapes.

It is important to make this investigation very "mistake-friendly." Students will certainly make mistakes: errors in counting, drawing, cutting and taping, labeling, and organizing. They may make several rectangles with the same area, but not all the possible rectangles. They may add incorrectly, especially if exploring shapes with a large area, such as 32 square units. In the first discussion, encourage students to find and address any errors that crop up, and simply point out how much sense making students must be doing to identify evidence that doesn't make sense. Celebrate the process of wrangling so much information to try to find patterns and think about relationships.

Activity

Launch

Launch this investigation by showing students a set of 12 square tiles scattered on the document camera. Ask students, What rectangles can I make using all of these tiles? Give students a moment to turn and talk to a partner. Collect some ideas and have students come up to move the tiles to create a couple of different rectangles. It will be useful if you can show more than one rectangle at the same time.

Ask students, Do all of these rectangles, made with the same area, have the same perimeter? Ask students to turn and talk to a partner and make a prediction, with a reason. Take some predictions. You might ask students to raise hands for who predicts they will be the same and who predicts they will be different. But most important, ask students to share some reasons behind their predictions.

Explore

Students investigate the following questions:

- Do all rectangles made with the same area have the same perimeter? Why or why not?
- If they do not have the same perimeter, what is the shortest perimeter possible for a particular area? What is the longest?

Invite partners to choose an area to investigate. We suggest starting with something between 10 and 36 square units. Provide partners with square tiles and grid paper (see appendix) to explore. For a given area, students create as many different rectangles as they can and determine their perimeters.

As students generate solutions for a given area, have them create a drawing for each on 1" grid paper (see appendix) including the area, the side lengths, and the perimeter. Provide copies of this large grid paper, scissors, and tape, as students will need to put together pieces to make long, narrow rectangles. Ask students to record the perimeter of each rectangle on the model they make.

Create a space on a wall or bulletin board where students can post their findings. At one end, label the space "Shortest Perimeter," and at the opposite end, label the space "Longest Perimeter." Add one additional label for "Area." This space will function like a giant table. Partners should post their rectangles, in order from shortest perimeter to longest perimeter, along with the area they explored.

Discuss

After students have generated a few rows on the class display, bring students together to study the evidence. Ask partners to turn and talk about what they notice. Ask, What patterns do you see? Give students a few minutes to talk. Bring partners back together to discuss what patterns they noticed. Ask, What conjectures can we make about these patterns? Record the class's conjectures on a chart or on the wall for students to think about and test. For instance, students may begin to notice that the long, skinny rectangles have the longest perimeter. You might record this as a conjecture: "The rectangles that are long and skinny, or have a side length of 1 unit, always have the longest perimeter." Although it is written as a statement, it is really a question that the class can test.

During this discussion, students may detect mistakes in the class's work: a rectangle out of place, an incorrect perimeter, or an inaccurate model. Encourage students to identify any places where they suspect a mistake, so they can investigate it and make a revision. Celebrate these opportunities to make, find, and revise mistakes.

Explore

Invite students to return to the investigation to:

- Generate more rows of the display.
- Fill in any gaps or address any errors that they think are in the table.
- Test the conjectures that most intrigue them.
- Identify any new patterns in rectangles with the same area.

Discuss

Gather students together where they can all see the growing display of rectangles they have created. Discuss the following questions:

- What patterns do we now notice?
- How did our conjectures hold up to investigation? What revisions can we make?
- How did organizing data in a table help us catch errors and address them?
- How are area and perimeter related?
- What kinds of shapes lead to the shortest perimeter? Why?
- What kinds of shapes lead to the longest perimeter? Why?

- If we didn't have to make rectangles, what shapes would you predict would have the shortest perimeter?

As you discuss these questions, revise your conjectures chart to reflect the class's current findings. Be sure to focus attention on the larger relationship between perimeter and area: as area gets more compact and closer to a square (or circle), the perimeter gets shorter; as area gets more spread out, the perimeter gets longer.

Look-Fors

- **Are students getting area and perimeter confused?** This is the first activity in which we have considered area and perimeter at the same time, and it is critical that students stay grounded in the two concepts. If you notice that students are struggling, which might sound like "Which one is perimeter?" support them in returning to experiences or references for perimeter that held meaning. You might remind students of the work they did surrounding objects with string, or hold your own arms out in a circle to physically model going around something. You might remind them of activities in which they were covering shapes with square tiles to find the area or space inside, as they did on the geoboard. You may want to make a chart for your classroom that explicitly names and describes these terms using the experiences that students have had with surrounding and covering.

- **Are students counting and constructing accurately?** Counting area and counting perimeter are different. As students toggle back and forth, they may get mixed up: Am I counting the edges or the squares? Pay attention to counting to make sure students count edges and tiles accurately. If you notice challenges, be sure to ask questions about what students are counting and why. Make sure students touch the parts they are counting if they get stuck or if they express doubt in calculating. When students move from making rectangles with tiles to drawing them on small or large grid paper, attend to how they count to make sure that their models all match. This is particularly difficult when student need to piece together a large rectangle using multiple pieces of the 1" grid paper. Encourage students to double-check their work and to label clearly.

- **Are students looking across their rectangles for patterns?** Students may make their rectangles in any order, but when they move toward posting their findings, support partners in doing a few things. First, students need to check that they think they have made all the possible rectangles. How do students know that they have made them all? Ask students questions about their process. Second, before they post their rectangles, they will need to order them by their perimeter, either on their table or, perhaps, on the floor. When they do this, ask them to take a moment to notice any patterns or to make observations. These are seeds of future discussion. Further, in laying them out, students may discover mistakes that they can address before posting.

- **How are students generating the rectangles that share an area?** Students may count out the appropriate number of tiles and simply begin to arrange them physically. Or you may notice that as they move the tiles, students seem to have some intent or idea for the rectangles they are making. You may begin to notice students thinking about multiplication when generating rectangles. Ask students questions about how they are making their rectangles, what patterns or ideas they are using, what helps them find new rectangles, and how they know when they have found them all. Be sure to draw attention to any use of multiplication, patterns of addition, or decomposing the numbers multiplicatively. For instance, if students say that they know they have made all the rectangles with an area of 15 square units because they know that 3×5 is the only way other than 1×15 to make 15, you'll want to ask why multiplication is a useful tool for finding area. If students say that they have made a rectangle with an area of 20 square units by making two 2×5 rectangles and putting them together, press students to explain why this works and what rectangles they can make this way. This is powerful multiplicative thinking that will serve students as flexible thinkers throughout their lives.

Reflect

If you had to make a shape with a long perimeter, what would it look like? Why?

Understanding $\frac{1}{2}$

Many students—and adults!—are confused by fractions, and it is not hard to understand why. Students are rarely introduced to fractions conceptually or visually, but instead are told that fractions are all about rules and methods that often make little sense. Students learn that when you multiply fractions, you multiply the numerator and the denominator, but that when you add fractions, you have to find common denominators and add the numerators. Division is another set of rules. These rules are often not based in understanding, so students try to memorize them. I have found in my teaching and work with students that the most important idea for students when learning fractions is the idea of a *relationship*. I teach students that what is special about a fraction is that the numerator relates to the denominator and that we do not know anything about the fraction without knowing what that relationship is. A fraction is big only if the numerator is a large proportion of the denominator, because the numerator and denominator are related. When students are taught rules about how to change the numerator and how to change the denominator, they start to see fractions as separate numbers and lose the critical idea of the relationship.

In this big idea, we help students see $\frac{1}{2}$ as a fractional relationship, at first asking them to make their own visual halves, so that they know that a half depends on the size of the whole that they choose. Inviting students to see halves visually is important, as the connection between numbers and visuals sparks brain connections that will help students understand fractions deeply.

In the Visualize activity, we provide students a chance to explore a piece of black-and-white art where they can discover and define their own halves of an area they define. In this activity, students define the whole and identify what part of it represents $\frac{1}{2}$. We think this will be a fun and exciting opportunity for students to expand on the idea that $\frac{1}{2}$ is a relational concept depending on both the numerator and the denominator. We have also included an additional piece of art with black, white, and gray shapes. In this activity, students will be able to further refine and define halves. For example, one student may draw a rectangle and say that the white and gray areas together make up half of the rectangle. The black area represents the other half. In these activities, students will see that a shaded area of a larger defined shape doesn't need to have all of the little areas connected. This is an important point for them to experience: $\frac{1}{2}$ is an area that can be in separate pieces.

The Play activity brings back our Number Visuals Sheet, which is a collection of dots representing the numbers 1–35 through factors. This visual representation of numbers is fascinating, and if students have not spent time with it before, they should take some time just to explore it and investigate what they see. In this activity, students will look for ways to represent half of each even number. They will notice that they cannot get an even number of dots in an odd-number visual pattern. This may lead to discussion about number and the idea of even and odd. As students identify their halves, they will be asked to record the way they see $\frac{1}{2}$ on a Number Visual Card. Students will see their own idea of $\frac{1}{2}$ in different ways. We encourage you to make a classroom display of the many different ways students see $\frac{1}{2}$ on the Number Visual Cards and especially the different ways they may see $\frac{1}{2}$ of the same number. As students work on this activity, they will be asked to think about what number $\frac{1}{2}$ represents for the number visuals they study. In the first activity, they think about $\frac{1}{2}$ as an area; in this activity, they see $\frac{1}{2}$ as a number. This variety in ways of seeing and understanding $\frac{1}{2}$ will help students learn $\frac{1}{2}$ more deeply.

In the Investigate activity, students will work to find a half of squares. Because some square numbers are even and some are odd, students will be breaking unit squares in half in some cases. The idea of even and odd will come up as possible conversation topics. We have emphasized students working in pairs and then sharing their ideas in different groups of four. We encourage this type of classroom activity because it promotes conversation, which is an important way for students to enhance their learning. Students will be sharing how they see and draw $\frac{1}{2}$ of a square, learning from the different visuals they see and the different conversations they have.

Jo Boaler

I Spy $\frac{1}{2}$

Snapshot

Students build a deep and flexible understanding of $\frac{1}{2}$ and whole by trying to spy $\frac{1}{2}$ in a complex geometric image.

> **Connection to CCSS**
> 3.NF.1, 3.NF.3a,b
> 3.G.2

Agenda

Activity	Time	Description/Prompt	Materials
Launch	5–10 min	Show students the I Spy $\frac{1}{2}$ Close-Up sheet and ask them where they see $\frac{1}{2}$ in the image. Students turn and talk and then share ideas. Model how to mark their thinking on the image, showing both the whole and the half.	I Spy $\frac{1}{2}$ Close-Up sheet, to display
Explore	20–30 min	Partners use the full-size I Spy $\frac{1}{2}$ sheet to find as many different ways to spy $\frac{1}{2}$ as they can. For each, they mark and label it on the image and then draw it on dot paper to make their thinking clearer.	• I Spy $\frac{1}{2}$ sheet, one per partnership • Dot paper (see appendix), at least one sheet per partnership • Colors
Discuss	15 min	Partners share the halves they found in the image, marking them on a sheet on the document camera and explaining how they knew it was $\frac{1}{2}$. Discuss the strategies students used and how they knew they were seeing $\frac{1}{2}$.	I Spy $\frac{1}{2}$ sheet, to display

(Continued)

Activity	Time	Description/Prompt	Materials
Extend	25–30 min	Students can try to spy $\frac{1}{2}$ on a more challenging image that includes three colors. For each $\frac{1}{2}$ they find, students mark and label it and then draw it on dot paper. Discuss how students' strategies changed when three colors were used.	• I Spy $\frac{1}{2}$: Challenge sheet, one per partnership • Dot paper (see appendix), at least one sheet per partnership • Colors

To the Teacher

The entry point for thinking about fractions is a deep understanding of $\frac{1}{2}$. In this activity, we play with finding $\frac{1}{2}$ in a geometric image, so that students can see $\frac{1}{2}$ as a relationship between the whole and the part. In this lesson, students cannot see $\frac{1}{2}$ without talking about what it is half *of*. Half can be 1 out of 2, but it can also be 4 parts out of 8 or 3 parts out of 6, or a triangle out of a square. Seeing $\frac{1}{2}$ flexibly, within a whole of different sizes, builds a foundation for thinking about fraction equivalence. We see this activity as a jumping-off point to noticing fractions in the world. Encourage students to share other places they spy $\frac{1}{2}$ and what it is $\frac{1}{2}$ of. They might begin to see that half of the windows in the classroom are closed or that half of the bulletin board is covered in green paper or that half of the students are wearing jeans.

In this image, $\frac{1}{2}$ can be seen in many places, once students start playing with the size and shape of the whole and are willing to decompose the pieces. A few examples are shown here.

A few examples of I Spy $\frac{1}{2}$. How many more can you find? *Source:* Image adapted from Shutterstock.com/sebos.

Later, to extend students' understanding of fractions to other unit fractions, you can use this same image again for exploring $\frac{1}{3}$ and $\frac{1}{4}$, or any other benchmark unit fraction. As the unit fractions get smaller, they become somewhat more challenging to spy in this image, but it works well through $\frac{1}{6}$.

Activity

Launch

Launch this lesson by showing students the I Spy $\frac{1}{2}$ Close-Up image, shown next, on a document camera. Ask students, Where can you see $\frac{1}{2}$? Give students a moment to turn and talk to a partner about where they see $\frac{1}{2}$ and how they know it is $\frac{1}{2}$.

Close-up image for class introduction and discussion. *Source:* Image adapted from Shutterstock.com/sebos.

Invite students to come up to the document camera to show where they see $\frac{1}{2}$. Be sure to ask students to be clear about the unit, or whole, they are using: $\frac{1}{2}$ *of* what? Where is the $\frac{1}{2}$? How do you know? As students point out their halves, mark the page by outlining the whole and labeling the $\frac{1}{2}$, showing students how to record their thinking. Take at least two different ideas from students, making sure that you've shown wholes of different sizes.

Explore

Provide partners with a copy of the I Spy $\frac{1}{2}$ sheet and colors to use to find as many different examples of $\frac{1}{2}$ as possible. Students outline the wholes and label the halves they find. Encourage students to come up with creative units and creative ways to construct $\frac{1}{2}$. Keep in mind that the $\frac{1}{2}$ does not need to be a single contiguous piece but can be constructed out of parts. This is an important concept for composing and decomposing shapes and fractions.

An example of $\frac{1}{2}$ where the pieces are not contiguous. *Source:* Image adapted from Shutterstock.com/sebos.

For every whole and $\frac{1}{2}$ students find, ask them to draw the whole and shade the $\frac{1}{2}$ on dot paper (see appendix). As you circulate around the classroom, be sure to ask students, How do you know each portion is $\frac{1}{2}$?

Discuss

Gather students together and show a copy of the I Spy $\frac{1}{2}$ sheet on the document camera. Ask students to share the different ways they saw $\frac{1}{2}$ in the image. Invite them to outline the whole, indicate $\frac{1}{2}$, and explain how they know. Celebrate creative and innovative solutions. Discuss the following questions:

- How did you know you were seeing $\frac{1}{2}$?
- What strategies did you use for constructing or testing whether a portion was $\frac{1}{2}$?

Be sure to highlight the strategies students used to compose pieces to make $\frac{1}{2}$, or count the components to confirm they had found $\frac{1}{2}$. Students will often intuitively count up triangles or squares of the whole and compare them to those that are gray and white. This counting and comparing is a useful stepping-stone toward equivalent fractions and gets at the relationship between whole and $\frac{1}{2}$. Students may also have mentally manipulated the pieces, moving them around in their minds until the gray and white look the same. This gets at the big idea about equal parts and should also be highlighted.

Extend

Offer students the black, gray, and white version of this image, which can be found on the I Spy $\frac{1}{2}$: Challenge sheet. Ask them to look for $\frac{1}{2}$ on this three-color version, which poses a new challenge. For instance, students might find a region that is $\frac{1}{2}$ black and $\frac{1}{2}$ gray and white together. This pushes students to think about $\frac{1}{2}$ and whole even more carefully. Again, ask students to record and be clear about where the $\frac{1}{2}$ is in their image by drawing it on dot paper (see appendix). Discuss the same questions and how their answers changed or evolved:

- How did you know you were seeing $\frac{1}{2}$?
- What strategies did you use for constructing or testing whether a portion was $\frac{1}{2}$?

Look-Fors

- **What kinds of halves are students noticing?** Some students may initially focus on halves that are familiar, those that have a rectangular whole and are divided into two congruent pieces, either triangles or rectangles. To challenge students to see $\frac{1}{2}$ in other ways, you might ask students, Can you find $\frac{1}{2}$ where the whole isn't a rectangle? Or, Can you find $\frac{1}{2}$ where the two halves are different shapes? Push students to think about whole and $\frac{1}{2}$ in flexible ways to deepen their understanding of what makes $\frac{1}{2}$.

- **Are students making connections to counting or decomposing the whole?** One way students can see $\frac{1}{2}$ and justify their thinking is to decompose the whole into pieces of the same size. In the case of this image, that typically means seeing the image as a series of identical triangles, or part of it as identical squares. Any region with the same number of equal-size parts that are gray and white would then be showing $\frac{1}{2}$. Students may do this intuitively; push them to articulate why seeing the region in pieces and counting those pieces helps them identify $\frac{1}{2}$. Also, pay attention for students who collect disconnected pieces to construct $\frac{1}{2}$. They are likely counting in some way. Ask them how they know they have found $\frac{1}{2}$, to help them construct an explanation they can share with the class in the discussion. These explanations may open the door to seeing equivalence, such as that 3 out of 6 pieces is the same as $\frac{1}{2}$, which is a bridge later to $\frac{3}{6} = \frac{1}{2}$.

Reflect

How can you see when something is $\frac{1}{2}$ of a whole?

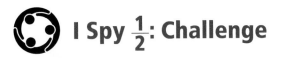 **I Spy $\frac{1}{2}$: Challenge**

Spotting $\frac{1}{2}$

Snapshot

Student play with finding half of numbers using the Number Visuals Sheet and look for patterns, connecting $\frac{1}{2}$ to even and odd, doubling, and equal groups.

Connection to CCSS
3.NF.1
3.NF.3a,b

Agenda

Activity	Time	Description/Prompt	Materials
Launch	10 min	Show students the Number Visual for 16 image and ask them to come up with as many ways to cut it in half as they can. Record these ways for all to see.	Number Visual for 16 sheet, to display
Play	20–25 min	Partners use the Number Visuals Sheet to figure out which numbers can be cut in half and which cannot (without cutting dots). Students find the value of $\frac{1}{2}$ wherever they can. Students look for multiple ways to cut numbers in half, color-coding or marking up the sheet to show their findings.	• Number Visuals Sheet, at least one per partnership • Colors
Discuss	15+ min	Discuss which numbers can be cut in half and collect students' findings on a class Number Visuals Sheet. Discuss the patterns students see in the numbers that can be cut in half and the values of $\frac{1}{2}$. Then record the multiple ways of cutting each number in half on Number Visual Cards. Create a display of these and look for patterns.	• Number Visuals Sheet, to display • Colors • Number Visual Card deck, multiple copies, cut apart, to display

To the Teacher

In this activity, we shift to looking at half of numbers rather than regions. The whole is given on the Number Visuals Sheet, but students now are challenged to determine when they can find $\frac{1}{2}$ of a number (without cutting the dots) and what the value of that $\frac{1}{2}$ is. You can extend this activity by asking students to predict a number they think they can find $\frac{1}{2}$ of, based on the patterns the class has discussed, and then ask them to create a visual for it that shows how to cut it in half. Students might choose, say, 40 or 56 or something even larger to play with.

Throughout the activity, look for opportunities to connect finding $\frac{1}{2}$ of a number with the concepts of addition, even and odd numbers, doubling, equal groups, and multiplication and division. These ideas are all related, and students may draw on their understanding of making equal groups to think about halving a set of dots or their notions of doubling as the inverse of halving. Note the connections students make and highlight these in the discussion so that everyone can see how these ideas are related and can help them think about fractions.

This activity can be repeated looking for other unit fractions. You can provide a Number Visuals Sheet to partners and ask them to look for numbers where they can find $\frac{1}{3}$ or $\frac{1}{4}$ or $\frac{1}{5}$ of that number without cutting the dots. This becomes a much more challenging task, but by repeating it the class can look at patterns across these different unit fractions. They might see, for instance, that they can find $\frac{1}{3}$ of every third number, and $\frac{1}{4}$ of every fourth number, and so on. They might also notice some numbers, such as 12, where they can find different fractions.

Activity

Launch

Launch this lesson by showing students the Number Visual for 16 image on the document camera, such as the one shown here. Ask students, Where do you see $\frac{1}{2}$? Give students a moment to think, and then facilitate as a number talk. Invite students to come up and show the different ways they see $\frac{1}{2}$. Record each new way of seeing $\frac{1}{2}$ on a different image of 16 on the sheet. Students might cut the image in half vertically or horizontally, or divide each cluster of four in half.

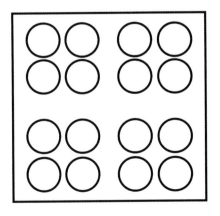

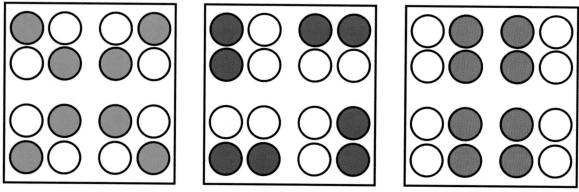

Our Number Visual for 16 with three examples of spotting $\frac{1}{2}$

They may find other creative ways to see $\frac{1}{2}$. Students may find it useful to both cut the image with lines and color in the circles in one half to make their thinking clear.

Tell students that today they will be playing with a set of number visuals for the numbers 1–35 and looking for as many different ways to find $\frac{1}{2}$ as they can.

Play

Provide partners with a copy of the Number Visuals Sheet and colors. Encourage students to begin by labeling each number, 1–35. Then partners try to find as many ways as they can to see $\frac{1}{2}$. Students explore the questions:

- In which numbers can you find $\frac{1}{2}$? Why?
- What is half of each of these numbers? Label the value of $\frac{1}{2}$, wherever you can.
- In which numbers can you find $\frac{1}{2}$ in multiple ways? Why?
- In which numbers can you not find $\frac{1}{2}$? Why? Students may suggest cutting dots in half. This is a creative solution! But you will want to encourage them to distinguish between the numbers where they have to cut dots in half and numbers where they do not have to cut dots to see $\frac{1}{2}$.

Students color-code or mark up their visuals to show $\frac{1}{2}$. They may need multiple copies of the Number Visuals Sheet to show seeing $\frac{1}{2}$ in the same number in different ways. Push students to label how they know when they have found $\frac{1}{2}$.

Discuss

Using a Number Visuals Sheet as a class record of students' thinking, discuss the following questions:

- Which of these numbers can show $\frac{1}{2}$ (without cutting dots in half)?
- What is $\frac{1}{2}$ of each of these numbers?
- How do we know when we have found them all?
- What patterns do you see?

As the class examines patterns, be sure they notice the alternating pattern of even (can be cut in half) and odd (cannot be cut in half) numbers. Also, discuss patterns in the values of $\frac{1}{2}$. For instance, $\frac{1}{2}$ of 2 is 1, $\frac{1}{2}$ of 4 is 2, $\frac{1}{2}$ of 6 is 3, and so on. The values of $\frac{1}{2}$ here form the counting sequence. Students may connect this to doubling, saying that double 1 is 2 and double 2 is 4. Students could use this to predict the value of $\frac{1}{2}$ of 36.

Then ask students, Which of the numbers can be cut in half in more than one way? Use the Number Visual Cards to record the multiple ways that students can cut the numbers in half. Post these multiple solutions on a board, ordered from smallest to largest. Then ask, What patterns do you notice in the numbers that can be cut in half more than one way? Again, there is an alternating pattern here, such that multiples of 4 can be cut in half more than one way, and the larger numbers can often be cut in half in multiple ways.

Look-Fors

- **What connections are students making to other number concepts as they find $\frac{1}{2}$?** As students explain their reasoning about how they are finding $\frac{1}{2}$ of the different numbers, they may connect the idea of halving to other concepts they know well, such as addition, even and odd numbers, doubling, equal groups, and multiplication and division. These connections may be explicit, such as a student saying, "I know 13 is half of 26 because 13 plus 13 is 26." In such cases you'll want to notice this connection out loud and ask students to share it in the discussion. You might say, "So, you're saying we know we've found half if you can add the two parts together and get back to the number we started with? Can you share that with the class?" Students might also make intuitive or implicit references to other concepts, such as saying that they found "a new way to divide it in half." When you notice these references to related concepts, ask students to talk about how they are related. You might ask, "I heard you say you divided the number in half. How is finding $\frac{1}{2}$ like division?" Again, invite students to share their thinking about these connections in the discussion. You could even create a concept map on a chart during the discussion showing all the conceptual connections students found to $\frac{1}{2}$.

- **Are students finding multiple ways to cut numbers in half?** Some students may focus on a single visual strategy for cutting in half, such as trying to partition the image vertically into two equal parts. However, not all the images that can be cut in half can be cut in this way. Further, there may be many other ways to visualize cutting in half, including cutting horizontally, cutting on an angle, or cutting smaller groups in half. Encourage students to look for different ways within each individual number they work with by asking, Is there another way to cut this number in half? If students think there is not, probe for why.

- **Are students cutting dots?** As noted earlier in the lesson, some students might find that all of the numbers can be cut in half as long as they can cut the dots themselves. This is true and should be honored as accurate. As teachers we sometimes make the mistake of telling students that the odd numbers are the ones that cannot be cut in half or shared in two groups equally. Mathematically, this is not true and can create conceptual challenges for students as they work with fractions. You'll want to ask any students who devise this strategy to share it with the class, and to try to name the value of $\frac{1}{2}$ when they use such a strategy. However, to investigate patterns, you will want to draw a distinction between those numbers for which we *must* cut a dot in half to make two equal groups and numbers for which we do not have to cut dots—that is to say, the numbers where $\frac{1}{2}$ is a whole number and numbers where $\frac{1}{2}$ includes a fraction. You might ask students to color-code these two kinds of numbers so that they can see and describe patterns.

Reflect

How can you predict what numbers you can find $\frac{1}{2}$ of?

Number Visual for 16

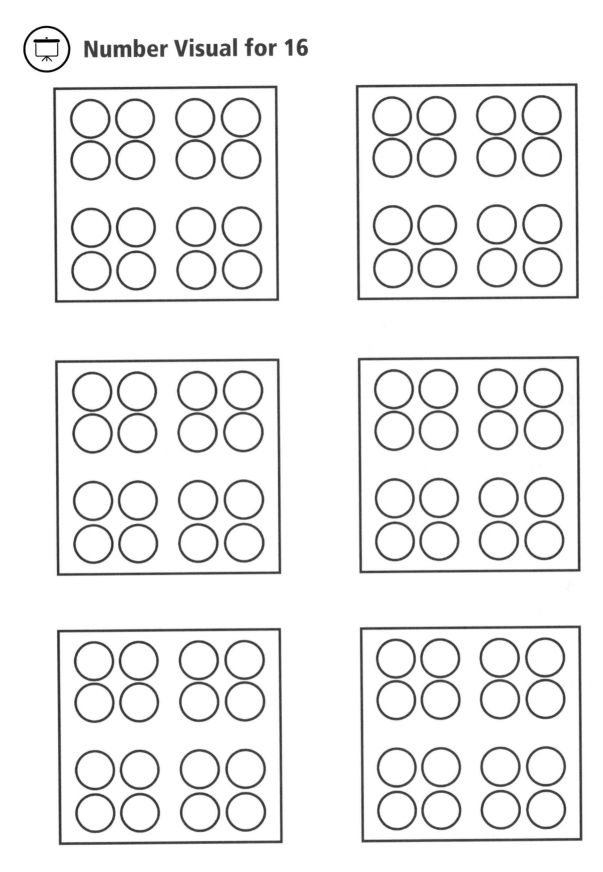

Number Visual Sheet

Number Visuals Cards

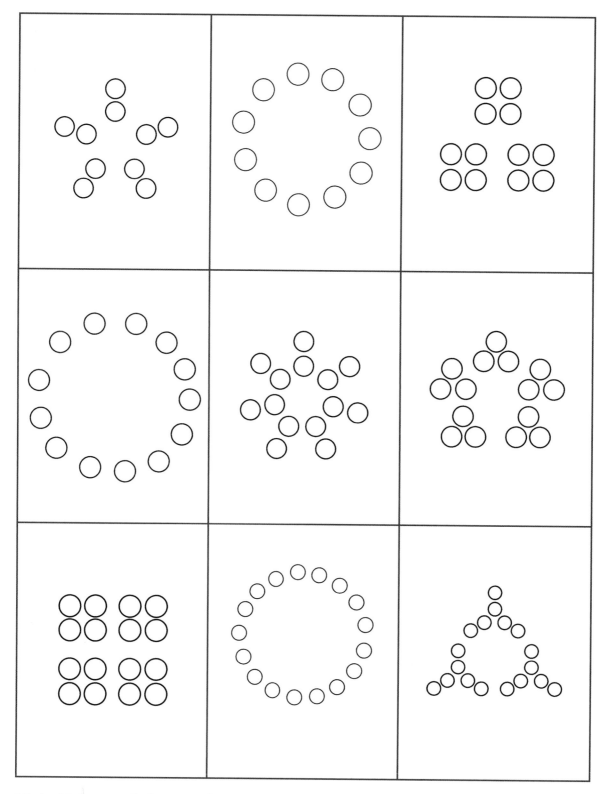

Number Visual Cards

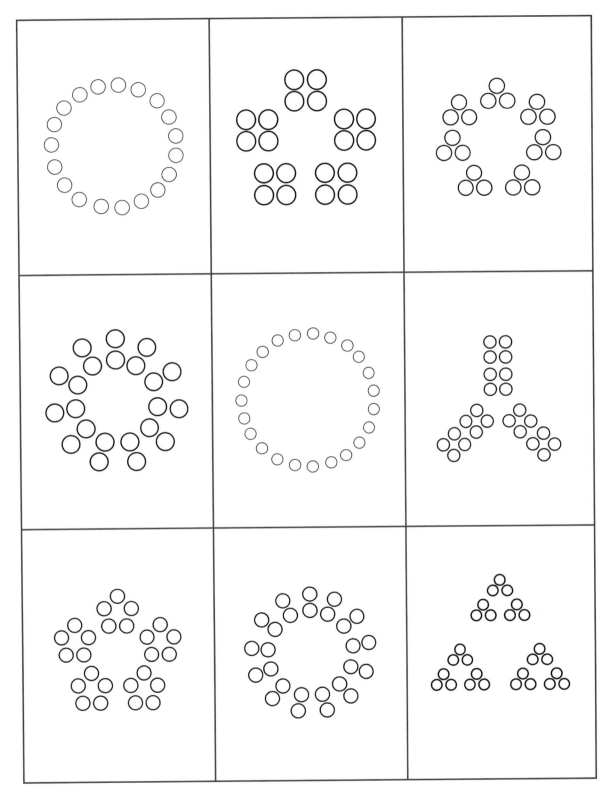

Number Visual Cards

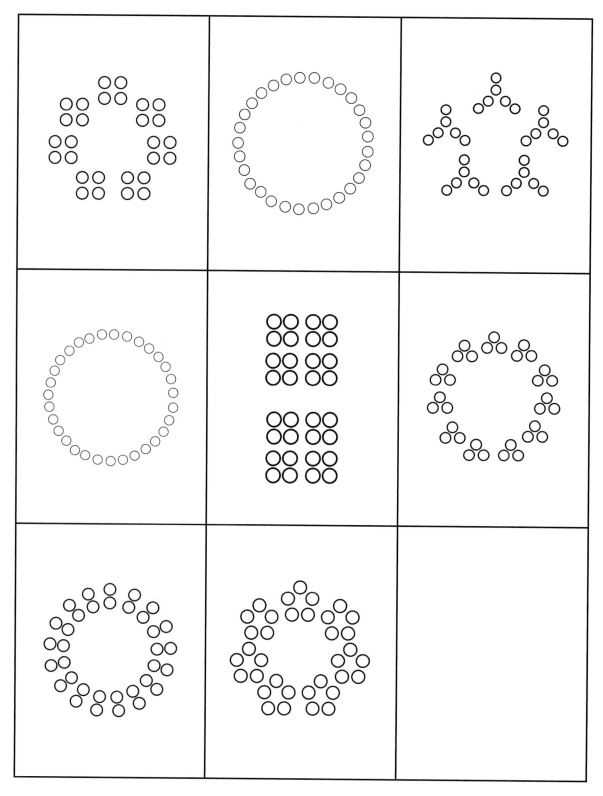

The Many Shapes of $\frac{1}{2}$

Snapshot

Students connect previous work with half of shapes and half of numbers to find half of the area of different sizes of squares. Students generate multiple ways to partition squares in half, justify those as half, and look for patterns.

Connection to CCSS
3.NF.1, 3.NF.3a,b
3.MD.5, 3.MD.6

Agenda

Activity	Time	Description/Prompt	Materials
Launch	10 min	Show students an 8 × 8 square board and provide partners with a copy. Ask students how they could cut this board in half. Invite students to share different ways, including ways that use a single line, multiple lines, patterning, and cutting individual squares in half.	8 × 8 Boards sheets, copied and cut in half, enough for one half-sheet per partnership and one to display
Explore	30+ min	Partners investigate different ways to cut square boards in half by looking at boards from 1 × 1 to 7 × 7. Students record their different ways on board sheets. Students investigate which boards can be cut in half the most ways and how they know they have cut a board in half. Students who want to investigate larger squares can do so with grid paper.	• Little Square Boards sheet, one or more per partnership • 4 × 4 Boards sheet, one or more per partnership • 5 × 5 Boards sheet, one or more per partnership • 6 × 6 Boards sheet, one or more per partnership • 7 × 7 Boards sheet, one or more per partnership • Colors • Optional: grid paper (see appendix)

(Continued)

Activity	Time	Description/Prompt	Materials
Discuss	15+ min	Pair two partnerships to discuss in groups of four the different ways of cutting squares in half. Then form new groups of four and repeat so that students get to see what others have found. As a whole class, discuss what strategies students had in common and what creative solutions students saw. Discuss how they know when they have found $\frac{1}{2}$ of a square. Generate questions students are wondering about based on what they found in this investigation.	Chart and markers
Extend	20+ min	If students generate compelling questions about fractions, $\frac{1}{2}$, or partitioning regions, investigate one or more of these questions as a class.	Optional: grid paper (see appendix), colors

To the Teacher

In this investigation, we take the ideas students have been exploring around the meaning of $\frac{1}{2}$ in the context of area models (Visualize activity) and number (Play activity) and merge the two to explicitly connect fractions to area. Students work together to find multiple ways to partition squares of different sizes into halves. Because the squares are on grids, it is possible to be precise about what $\frac{1}{2}$ of the square is, and students can count the areas of the regions they create to prove that they have found $\frac{1}{2}$. We encourage you to look for opportunities to connect the language students learned when exploring area to this investigation.

Encourage students to get creative about partitioning in multiple ways to represent $\frac{1}{2}$ of the squares. There are many, many potential solutions for each size of square, and this investigation deepens as student develop innovative solutions. Celebrate out-of-the-box thinking!

We have provided many sheets with squares of different sizes for students to explore. The advantage of these is that they come prepartitioned into square units, and students can dive right into $\frac{1}{2}$. However, this investigation can be conducted using square paper, such as origami paper. Students can create squares of any dimensions by folding the paper into rows and columns of any number. Students can then partition these squares by cutting away half and pasting the partitioned square onto a black piece of construction paper for a vivid display. If you choose to use this alternative form of exploration, students will likely move through far fewer squares during the time you have for the activity, but they will get lots of work with partitioning and thinking about equal area as they fold rows and columns.

Activity

Launch

Launch this investigation by showing students a copy of one of the squares on the 8 × 8 Boards sheet on the document camera. Ask students, How could we cut this square in half? Give each pair of students a copy of one of the 8 × 8 Boards half-sheets. Give students a moment to look at the image with a partner and come up with at least one way of cutting it in half. Encourage them to draw their way(s) on the sheet.

Ask for students' ideas for different ways to cut the board in half. Invite students to come up to show their ways. Be sure to highlight ways that use a single straight line on the grid line, use multiple lines (such as a zigzag), pattern the square (like a checkerboard), and cut squares in half, if students find these different kinds of strategies.

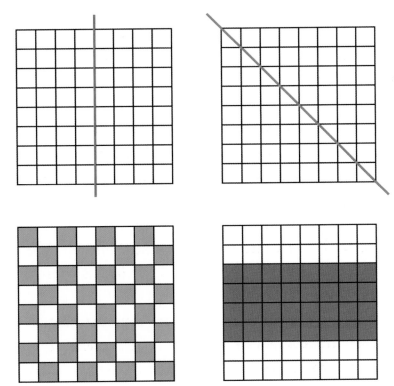

Examples of an 8 × 8 square grid cut in half

Tell students that today they will be investigating different ways to cut square boards of different sizes in half and that their goal is to find as many different ways as possible.

Explore

Provide each partnership with one copy each of the Little Square Boards sheet, 4×4 Boards sheet, 5×5 Boards sheet, 6×6 Boards sheet, and 7×7 Boards sheet. Students may ultimately want multiple copies of these sheets if they find lots of ways to cut the squares in half. Provide students with colors to use to show their thinking. Partners explore different ways they can cut square boards of different sizes in half. Students investigate the following questions:

- How can we cut each square in half?
- Which squares can be cut in half in the most ways? Why?
- What is $\frac{1}{2}$ of each square?
- How do you know that you have cut the square in half? What are your strategies for justifying that you have $\frac{1}{2}$?

For each way students find to cut a square in half, they should record it on one of the board sheets. If students would like to investigate larger-size squares after exploring 1×1 through 7×7 squares, provide students with grid paper (see appendix) to use to draw their own squares.

Discuss

Begin the discussion in small groups by pairing up the partnerships into groups of four. Ask partners to share with one another the different ways they found to cut the square boards in half. Students should discuss the following questions:

- What did we do that was similar? What strategies do we have in common?
- What did we do that was different? (Encourage kids to celebrate creativity!)

Now ask partners to rotate so that new groups of four are created and they can share with a different pair of students, focusing their discussion on the same questions.

Finally, bring everyone together to discuss the following questions:

- What strategies do we share? What ways of cutting boards in half were common?
- Do we have any mistakes to celebrate? (Invite students to share and revise.)
- What were the most creative ways you saw? What did you see that surprised you?
- What is $\frac{1}{2}$ of each square? Why does that make sense?
- What patterns did you notice in our solutions?
- What are you wondering now? (Spend some time generating questions based on this investigation. Record these questions on a chart.)

In this part of the discussion, be sure to note connections students make to area. For instance, students might say that $\frac{1}{2}$ of the 4×4 square is 8. Push students to use language to label that as "8 square units" and ask why this makes sense. Encourage connection to the area of the larger square being 16 square units, so that any method of partitioning the square that results in 8 square units in a region is $\frac{1}{2}$ of 16 square units.

Extend

If students arrive at interesting questions about $\frac{1}{2}$ or square boards in the closing discussion, we encourage you to pursue their questions. For instance, students might wonder what might happen if you tried to cut the board into thirds or fourths, or they may be intrigued about what would happen if the boards were not square. Provide students with grid paper (see appendix) and colors to investigate the most compelling questions students generate and then discuss what students find.

Look-Fors

- **How are students connecting $\frac{1}{2}$ to area?** Look for any opportunities to make explicit connections to area and the language we use to describe the area of rectangles. Students may use counting to justify when they have found $\frac{1}{2}$, as in, "There are 2 here and 2 here, so it's $\frac{1}{2}$." When you hear these kinds of explanations, push students to explain, 2 what? These are the square units of the area of the larger square, and when students have found $\frac{1}{2}$, they have found a way to show $\frac{1}{2}$ of the area of that square. Try to use the language of area when you talk with students. You might ask questions such as, "How do you know that the area of this shape is $\frac{1}{2}$ the area of the square?"

- **Are students thinking flexibly about the different ways they can partition a square into halves?** There are many different ways to approach partitioning the square into halves. Students often start most readily with a single line vertically, horizontally, or, perhaps, diagonally. But they may need some prompting to look for solutions that use multiple line segments, such as a zigzag, or solutions, such as the diagonal line, that do not adhere to the grid line. Even more creative can be solutions that simply treat each square unit inside the larger square as a region to be shared. Students might make the connection to area and realize that any solution in which $\frac{1}{2}$ of the square units are colored is a valid representation of $\frac{1}{2}$. If students say they think they have found all the possible solutions, be sure to push them by asking, Can you find another way? You may want to point out any assumptions they are making that they could question, such as, "I notice that you have followed the grid line in all your solutions. Could you make $\frac{1}{2}$ without following the grid?"

- **Are students noticing and using systems to generate solutions?** As students move from one size square to the next, they may begin to use similar strategies that they repeat again and again. For instance, students might start with all the single-line solutions, cutting the square vertically, horizontally, and diagonally. Then they might have some patterns they use to construct zigzag solutions by using multiple lines. This is the beginning of having a system for finding solutions. If you notice partnerships where the first few solutions for each square size are similar, ask questions about the systems they are developing for finding solutions. You might ask whether these systems always work, and if they don't, when they do not work. For instance, students might say that there are different solutions for squares with even side lengths than for odd side lengths. Alternatively, students might say there is no difference at all based on even or odd, but that larger squares require more and more solutions so that their systems have to get bigger or more elaborate each time. Prompt students to talk about how they are reasoning about these solutions and the systems they are creating.

Reflect

What does $\frac{1}{2}$ mean? Tell or show as many different ways of thinking about $\frac{1}{2}$ as you can.

8 × 8 Boards

Little Square Boards

 **5 × 5 Boards**

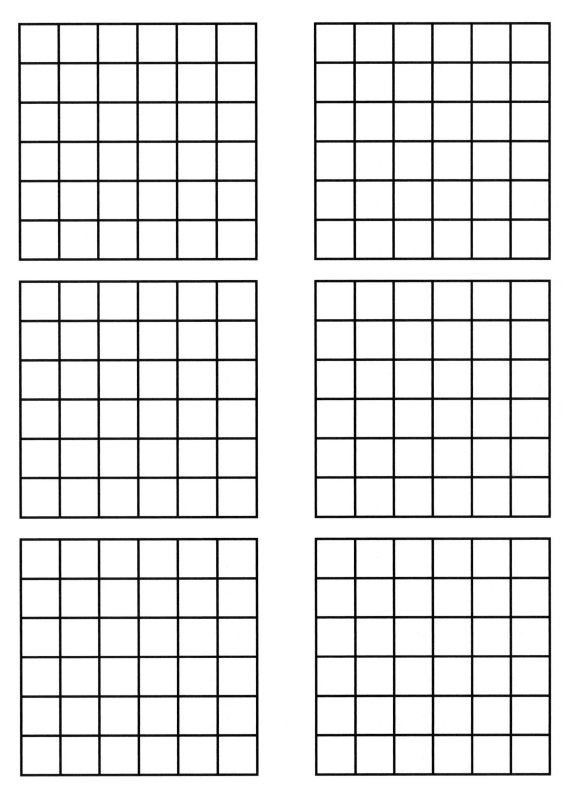

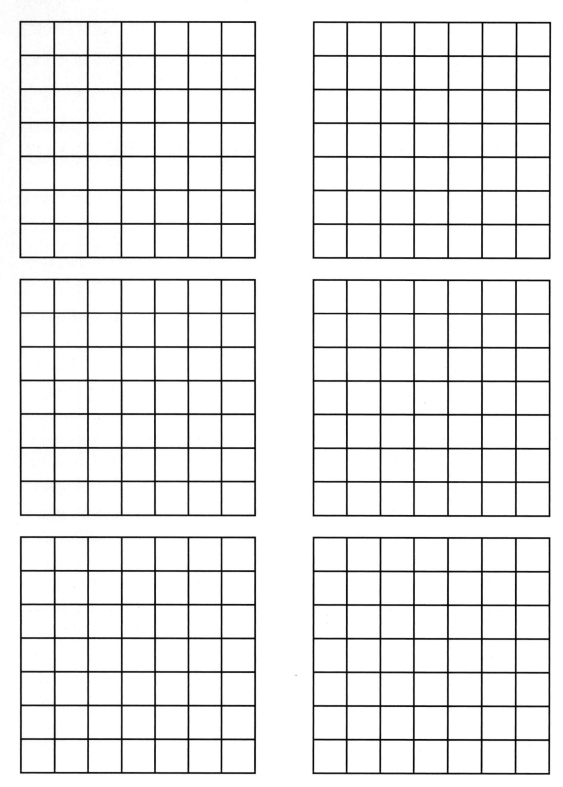

BIG IDEA 7

Seeing Fractions: The Parts and the Wholes

In this big idea, we expand to other unit fractions, beyond $\frac{1}{2}$, again inviting students to see and make their own fractions. We also introduce students to fractions as a linear measurement and to numbers decomposed into fractional parts. This fraction work is designed to be challenging, as it is only when we are struggling that we are truly learning. It is important for both teachers and students to embrace and value times of struggle. As teachers we often try to save students from struggle, jumping in and showing them what to do or breaking work down for them. Instead of doing this, it is better to share mindset messages and to tell students that struggle is really good and essential for brain growth. In this big idea, we have provided many opportunities to celebrate the different ways students come up with visuals and other types of solutions, as well as times of struggle.

In the Visualize activity, students are asked to analyze shapes that are formed from different pattern blocks. They will be asked to see different fractions inside each image. One of the shapes inside each pattern block is an equilateral triangle that can be thought of as one unit. This discovery should be left to the students—once they have seen the equilateral triangle, they will start to see the ways other blocks can be made up from this base unit shape. The idea of breaking a whole into equal-size units to express fractions is a central one in mathematics and one that is worthy of some discussion with the students.

In the Play activity, we bring back the black-and-white triangle-and-square image from a previous lesson. Here students use the triangle-and-square grids again to play a cooperative game in which they work together to cover the entire game board as they identify unit fractions of a region they define. Students will choose their region and their unit to count by, a square or a triangle. As students progress, they will begin to define areas that are not rectangles but other more complex shapes. There are lots of opportunities here for students to discuss unit fractions $\frac{1}{1}$ through $\frac{1}{6}$, because they roll a single die to determine the unit fraction they will define.

In the Investigate activity, we revisit perimeter. Students are asked to find rectangles that have an odd-number perimeter. They will need to think creatively and will most likely make mistakes. We start with an odd number, 17, and ask students to construct rectangles that have a perimeter of 17. Students will discover that they need to use fractional side lengths. They move forward to consider other even- and odd-number perimeters. As they decompose a whole number into fractional parts to determine different rectangles that have a perimeter of 17, students may start to question the notion of infinity. This is a great opportunity to discuss how many different ways we might make rectangles with a perimeter of 17.

Jo Boaler

Seeing Parts and Wholes

Snapshot

Students explore unit fractions and the relationship between part and whole by creating visual models using pattern blocks.

> Connection to CCSS
> 3.NF.1, 3.NF.3a
> 3.G.2, 3.MD.6

Agenda

Activity	Time	Description/Prompt	Materials
Launch	10 min	Show students a simple figure made from pattern blocks like the examples provided. Ask students, What fractions do you see? What fraction names can you give to these fractions? Come to agreement as a class on fraction names that make sense.	Shape made from pattern blocks, to display
Explore	30+ min	Partners use pattern blocks to create figures that show each of the unit fractions $\frac{1}{2}$, $\frac{1}{3}$, $\frac{1}{4}$, $\frac{1}{5}$, $\frac{1}{6}$, and $\frac{1}{8}$. For each image they create, they record it on isometric dot paper, along with a visual proof of the fraction name they have given to that part of the image. Students post these images in a display space, sorted by unit fraction.	• Pattern blocks, for each partnership • Pattern Block Isometric Dot Paper sheets, multiple copies per partnership • Colors • Scissors • Display space for posting student work, labeled with unit fraction names
Discuss	15+ min	Looking at the class display of unit fractions, ask students to focus on images of one unit fraction, such as $\frac{1}{3}$. Ask, What do these representations have in common? How do they show $\frac{1}{3}$? What makes $\frac{1}{3}$? Discuss another fraction's images with similar questions. Record students' ways of describing fractions on a chart.	Optional: chart and markers

To the Teacher

To prepare for this lesson, set up six different spaces for students to post solutions, each with a header: $\frac{1}{2}$, $\frac{1}{3}$, $\frac{1}{4}$, $\frac{1}{5}$, $\frac{1}{6}$, and $\frac{1}{8}$. This can be a bulletin board, wall, or spot on a whiteboard. Make sure there is enough space for many student solutions. You can also set up another space for other fractions students find. Students can post other unit fractions, such as $\frac{1}{7}$, or nonunit fractions like $\frac{2}{3}$ or $\frac{3}{4}$.

The big idea here is that a fraction is a relationship between the part and the whole. No shape in the pattern blocks is in itself $\frac{1}{4}$. It is only $\frac{1}{4}$ of something larger. The same shape can be $\frac{1}{4}$ or $\frac{1}{3}$ or $\frac{1}{2}$, depending on the whole.

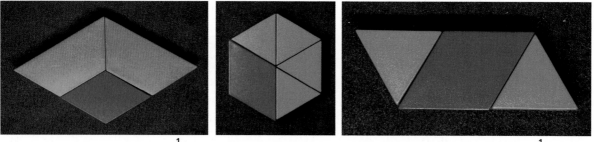

The blue rhombus represents $\frac{1}{4}$ of the entire shape.

The blue rhombus represents $\frac{1}{3}$ of the entire shape.

The blue rhombus represents $\frac{1}{2}$ of the entire shape.

We have provided large isometric dot paper that matches the size of typical pattern blocks to support students in recording the images they create. Students can lay their pattern blocks directly on the dot paper to make transferring easier and so that they can check that the recording they make matches the figure they constructed out of blocks.

Activity

Launch

Launch the activity by building a simple shape on the document camera using at least three different pattern blocks. We've provided a few examples in the figure here. Note that these examples can be decomposed into sixths and eighths, which are friendly fractions. We encourage you to avoid constructing shapes based on ninths or other less friendly units.

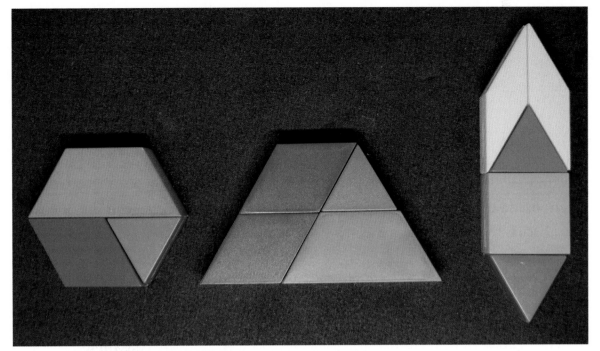

Examples of pattern block figures you could show students

Ask students, Where do you see fractions? What fractions do you see? Ask students to turn and talk to a partner about the fractions they see and what fraction names they would give to them. Invite students to come up and show the different fractions they see. Ask, What fraction name would you give to the part you've shown? Why does that fraction name make sense? Be sure that the class can agree on the fraction names that can be used for the different parts students point out. Tell students that today they will be exploring how to make images from pattern blocks for different fractions and how to prove that the fraction names make sense.

Explore

Partners construct models for each unit fraction $\frac{1}{2}$, $\frac{1}{3}$, $\frac{1}{4}$, $\frac{1}{5}$, $\frac{1}{6}$, and $\frac{1}{8}$ using pattern blocks. For each example that they create, students draw and label their fraction on Pattern Block Isometric Dot Paper sheets. Students use their images to construct visual proofs for the fraction name they are giving to the parts. Using lines, arrows, numbers, or other labels, students show evidence that the model they've created shows $\frac{1}{2}$, $\frac{1}{3}$, $\frac{1}{4}$, $\frac{1}{5}$, $\frac{1}{6}$, or $\frac{1}{8}$. Note that any image students create can show multiple fractions, depending on which part of the figure students label. Students should make clear which part of the drawing represents the unit fraction they are modeling. For each model they create, students cut out and post their solution with their evidence on the class display space you've set up.

Students are welcome to explore nonunit fractions as well, provided that they can show them as the sum of unit fractions. For instance, if a group creates a model for $\frac{3}{4}$, they need to show how $\frac{3}{4}$ is three regions that are each $\frac{1}{4}$ of the whole. These can be posted in another area of the class display.

Discuss

Gather students together near the class display and ask them to look at the solutions for one of the unit fractions. We suggest $\frac{1}{3}$ as an interesting place to start. If you choose to begin with a different fraction, swap out the language in the questions here. Discuss the following:

- What do the representations of $\frac{1}{3}$ have in common?
- How do you know each one is $\frac{1}{3}$?
- What makes $\frac{1}{3}$?

Be sure to draw students' attention to the relationship between the parts and the whole. One-third is a relationship between the part and the whole. For instance, the red trapezoid is $\frac{1}{3}$ only when the whole is three times the size of the trapezoid. As you discuss these question, you may want to write down the language students use to describe fractions on a chart to use for reference in future work. Repeat this discussion with a different fraction, such as $\frac{1}{6}$ or $\frac{1}{8}$. Again, focus on what makes that fraction and the relationship between the part and whole, and add to your chart as students describe ways of seeing fractions.

Look-Fors

- **Are students thinking about the number or the size of the pieces?** When students are working with pattern blocks, one major conceptual challenge is that the pieces are different sizes. Students can construct fractions by iterating the same-size unit. For instance, $\frac{1}{5}$ can be constructed by making a figure out of five triangles and pointing out one of them. However, if students use different-size pieces, as shown in the launch, they will need to think about their relative size to determine the fraction a piece represents. For instance, if a triangle is next to a rhombus, the triangle is $\frac{1}{3}$ of the figure, even though that figure is made of only two pieces. This activity pushes students to grapple with whether fractions are about area or number. You might want to slow down on these conversations to ask, Why does the number of pieces matter?

Why does the size of the pieces matter? How do we decide which to pay attention to?

- **Are students recognizing that the fraction names part of the image, rather than the whole image?** As students use the images they create to represent different unit fractions, it is important that students recognize that only part of their image shows a particular unit fraction. The image they create might "show $\frac{1}{4}$," but students should be precise about which part of the image is $\frac{1}{4}$ of the whole. If students use this language, ask, Where in this image can we see $\frac{1}{4}$? Which part is $\frac{1}{4}$? How do you know?

- **How are students decomposing the figures to determine what fractions they see or can make?** To see or construct unit fractions from the pattern blocks, students need to decompose larger blocks in terms of a smaller unit. The triangle is the universal unit in the pattern blocks; most of the other blocks can be expressed as multiples of the triangle, and the beige rhombus is the same size as the triangle. When building with these shapes, it is useful to think about the blue rhombus as two triangles, the trapezoid as three triangles, and the hexagon as six triangles. Decomposing creates a shared unit, which is necessary for determining the unit fraction. Students will have difficulty when using the square, because it does not readily fit into this system, and this is a productive idea for students to discover as they work. Ask questions about how students know what the unit fraction is and how they saw the parts of their figure when they were thinking about fractions. Encourage students to include this decomposition in their visual proofs, and you will want to bring up the relationships between the pieces in the discussion wherever the opportunity arises.

Reflect

What kind of shape can you make where the blue rhombus is $\frac{1}{3}$? How could you change the shape so that the blue rhombus becomes a different fraction?

Pattern Block Isometric Dot Paper

Cover, Cut, and Sort

Snapshot

In the game Cover Up, students play with finding unit fractions in a complex geometric image and work together to try to cover the board. Then they cut out the shapes they made and sort them by unit fractions to explore patterns and develop strategies for playing the game.

Connection to CCSS
3.NF.1, 3.NF.3a-c
3.G.2, 3.MD.6

Agenda

Activity	Time	Description/Prompt	Materials
Launch	10–15 min	Show students the Cover Up Close-Up image and ask where they see $\frac{1}{6}$. Take student ideas and reasoning. Model how to play Cover Up on this board by rolling the die and marking areas on the board that correspond to the unit fraction with the denominator rolled.	• Cover Up Close-Up sheet, to display • Marker • Die
Play	20–30 min	Students play Cover Up in groups of two or three. Students work together to try to completely cover the board with unit fractions. The game is over when the board is covered or no one can find the fraction rolled. Students may play with one of three boards to vary the challenge.	• Cover Up Close-Up or Cover Up Game Board, multiple copies per partnership • Dice, one per partnership • Colors
Discuss	10–15 min	Discuss the strategies students developed for playing the game and the patterns they noticed along the way. Ask students which fractions were easier or harder to find and discuss why this may be.	

Explore	20 min	Students cut out the regions they found on their game boards and sort them by unit fraction. Students tape or glue these onto the Unit Fraction Sort sheets so they can see all the shapes that show the same fraction. Partners explore the patterns they notice and how these might help them play the game.	• Unit Fraction Sort sheets, set of two per partnership • Scissors • Glue or tape
Discuss	10 min	Discuss the patterns students notice in their sorts and how these might help them to play the game strategically.	
Extend	20–40 min	Partners revisit the game to play using the strategies the class developed in the discussion. Students may then create their own game boards based on what they have learned makes the game more or less challenging.	• Cover Up Close-Up or Cover Up Game Board, multiple copies per partnership • Dice, one per partnership • Colors • Optional: dot paper (see appendix), sheet protectors, and dry erase markers

To the Teacher

In this game, we return to versions of the image used in the Visualize activity in Big Idea 6, I Spy $\frac{1}{2}$. Students can draw on their experience with this image focusing on $\frac{1}{2}$ to extend their thinking to other unit fractions. The focus of this game is to grapple with the relationship between part and whole, and to dig into how fractions can be composed and decomposed using these parts and wholes. As students are playing the game, they need to agree on the moves that their partners make. That is, everyone needs to be convinced that the player has indeed found the unit fraction they claim they have, and their justification should be convincing to everyone. Just as in I Spy $\frac{1}{2}$, the regions students mark do not need to be rectangular, and the parts that represent the unit fraction do not need to be contiguous. Some examples of accurate and justifiable representations of different unit fractions are shown here.

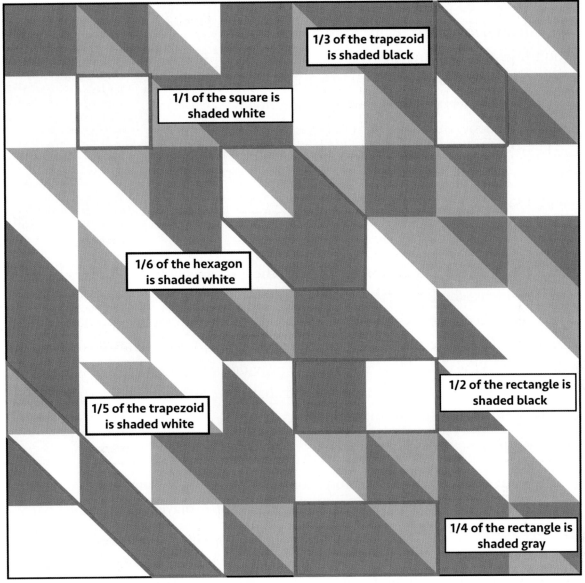

1/3 of the trapezoid is shaded black

1/1 of the square is shaded white

1/6 of the hexagon is shaded white

1/2 of the rectangle is shaded black

1/5 of the trapezoid is shaded white

1/4 of the rectangle is shaded gray

Source: Image adapted from Shutterstock.com/sebos.

Activity

Launch

Launch the activity by showing students the Cover Up Close-Up image on a document camera. This is a portion of the full Cover Up Game Board. If students have used a version of this image in I Spy $\frac{1}{2}$, then you may want to remind them of how they used the picture to find different ways of representing that fraction. Tell students that they are going to be using this image in a different way today to find fractions. Ask students, Where do you see $\frac{1}{6}$? Give students a chance to turn and talk to a partner, then take some ideas. Be sure to push students to justify their examples of $\frac{1}{6}$ by showing the whole and the portion that represents $\frac{1}{6}$ of that whole.

Model how the game Cover Up is played, by rolling a die and inviting students to come up and find on the game board the unit fraction with the denominator rolled. Show students how to mark off and label their whole and the unit fraction they found. Tell students that the goal is to cover the entire board and that the game ends either when the board is covered or when they cannot find the fraction they roll.

Source: Image by Shutterstock.com/ Milissa4like.

Play

Students play Cover Up in pairs or trios, with the goal of covering the entire board together. Students should feel free to coach one another on good moves to achieve this goal, as it is a cooperative game. Alternatively, the game can be played solo with the same goal. We suggest starting with the Cover Up Close-Up game board, which you displayed to the class. However, we have provided two larger boards, one with two and one with three colors, for additional challenge. Students may start with one size and change to another during the activity.

Game Directions

- To play, each group will need one copy of a Cover Up Game Board (or the Cover Up Close-Up sheet), one different color per player to mark the board, and one die.

- Players take turns. On a turn, roll the die. The number shown on the die is the denominator of a unit fraction. For instance, a roll of 2 represents $\frac{1}{2}$. A roll of 5 represents $\frac{1}{5}$. A roll 1 represents $\frac{1}{1}$ or a whole.

- The player now marks a single region on the game board where they see the fraction they have rolled represented. The region can be any shape. For instance, if the player rolled 4, they would

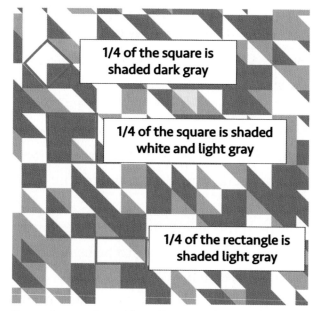

1/4 of the square is shaded dark gray

1/4 of the square is shaded white and light gray

1/4 of the rectangle is shaded light gray

Source: Image adapted from Shutterstock.com/Milissa4like.

look for a region that showed $\frac{1}{4}$, such as the one shown in the figure on the previous page. To the Teacher shows additional examples.

- The player marks the region and labels it with the fraction using his or her own color.
- Play continues, taking turns until one of the following happens:
  - The entire board is covered! All players win!
  - A player rolls a number and, with help from the other players, cannot find that fraction represented on the board. Count the number of squares left on the board. Play again and try to end with fewer unmarked squares.

Discuss

Discuss as a class the following questions:
- What strategies did you develop for playing the game?
- How did you see the fractions?
- What fractions were easier or harder to find? Why?
- Did you notice any patterns as you played the game?

Draw attention to strategies that focus on decomposing into common units, such as squares or triangles. Focus on the wholes and the parts that students were seeing in relationship to one another.

Explore

Ask partners to cut up their game board(s) into the different shapes they made. Students sort their shapes into those that represent $\frac{1}{1}$, $\frac{1}{2}$, $\frac{1}{3}$, $\frac{1}{4}$, $\frac{1}{5}$, and $\frac{1}{6}$. Students glue or tape these down onto the Unit Fraction Sort sheets under the headings for each fraction. Students explore the following questions:

- What patterns do you see in the shapes you made?
- How might these patterns help you play the game?

Discuss

Discuss the fraction sort students have created and what they noticed:

- What patterns did you notice in the shapes that made the same fraction?
- How might these patterns help you play the game?

Be sure to support students in shifting from what they noticed to how they might use that to play the game more strategically. Students may come up with ideas about more advantageous sizes for the whole, the placement of fractions on the board, or how to manage the end of the game.

Extend

Students can revisit the game using the strategies and patterns they noticed and discussed as a class. We encourage you to return to the same game boards students played with in the activity. But then students can make their own game boards using dot paper (see appendix). You can either photocopy these for students to play with or slip the original into a page protector and use dry erase markers so that these constructed boards can be used repeatedly. Encourage students to think about their own experience with the provided boards when designing their own. You might ask, What makes a game board harder or easier? How big do you think it needs to be? How many colors will you use? What will be the smallest unit on your board?

Look-Fors

- **How are students seeing the fractions?** Students will need to decompose in two ways to be able to see fractions on the game board. First, they need to see parts of the game board that they might use. Second, they need to think about the components of the regions they choose by choosing a unit, such as a triangle or square, that can be used to compose the region and the unit fraction. These units are key to locating and representing unit fractions. Ask students to explain how they see the fractions, what the unit is, and how that unit relates to the whole. We encourage you to use the language of *unit, unit fraction, decompose,* and *compose* to describe what students are doing and help them articulate what they are seeing as they look for fractions.

- **How are students adjusting the regions they find to fit the unit fraction they roll?** Students may search the board for places that look like good candidates for the unit fraction they roll. But what are they doing if the region doesn't quite fit? For instance, if a student rolls $\frac{1}{5}$ and sees a region that ends up showing $\frac{1}{4}$, how do they respond to being close? Students can revise the region they have found by adding new parts to it to make it larger, or by cutting sections off of it to make it smaller. These revisions represent deep thinking about what makes a fraction, how to decompose, and the relationship between part and whole. Encourage students to slow down on these moments of revision and talk with you about their reasoning. You may want to support students by asking, What could you do to this shape to make it show your fraction?

- **Are student thinking strategically about the game?** Pay attention to the ways that students are placing their fractions on the board, and how their strategies develop over game play. Encourage students to reflect with you about what they are learning as they play and to talk about strategy within their groups. This is a cooperative game in which students win or lose together, so sharing strategies and talking about better moves support both learning and game play. That said, it is important that each player gets a chance to think about how and where to locate fractions without others rushing their thinking or diminishing their ideas. Support groups in balancing each student's chance to make mistakes and the group's opportunity to discuss and debate ideas.

Reflect

If you were teaching someone how to play Cover Up, what is one strategy you think they ought to know? Why?

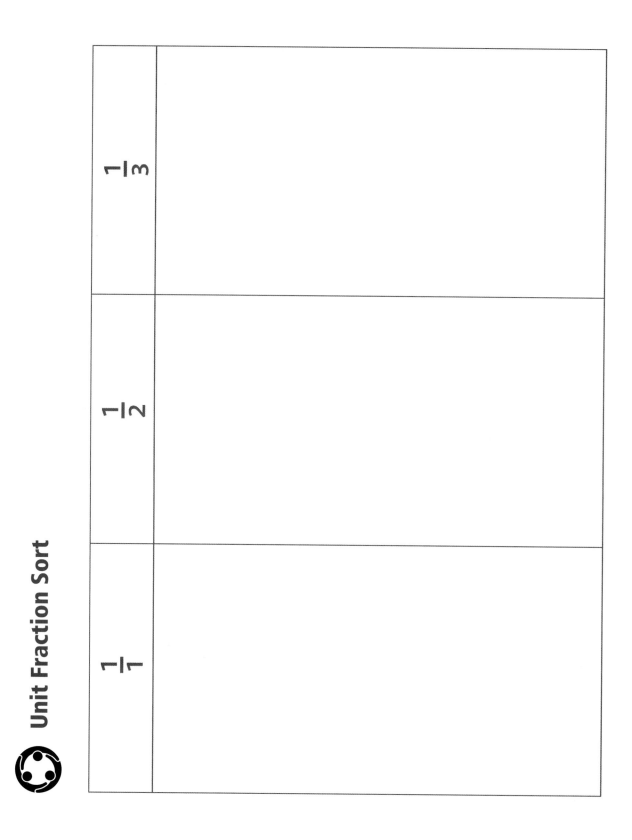

Unit Fraction Sort

$\dfrac{1}{1}$	$\dfrac{1}{2}$	$\dfrac{1}{3}$

Unit Fraction Sort

$\dfrac{1}{4}$	$\dfrac{1}{5}$	$\dfrac{1}{6}$

Taking a Fractional Walk

Snapshot

Students connect fractions to distance and the number line by finding as many different rectangles as they can with a perimeter of 17 units.

Connection to CCSS
3.NF.1, 3.NF.2
3.MD.8

Agenda

Activity	Time	Description/Prompt	Materials
Launch	10 min	Brainstorm with students different rectangles with a perimeter of 12 units. Invite students to share the rectangles they come up with and explain their perimeter. Then ask students, What rectangles have a perimeter of 17 units?	Chart and markers, or grid paper (see appendix), to display
Explore	25–30 min	Partners investigate the rectangles they can make with a perimeter of 17 units. Students record any rectangles they make.	• Grid or dot paper (see appendix), for each partnership • Square tiles
Discuss	15+ min	Discuss the different rectangles with a perimeter of 17 units that students found. Students justify the perimeter. Celebrate creative solutions, discuss what made finding rectangles challenging, and focus on the need for fractional side lengths. Discuss whether it is possible to find all the rectangles with a perimeter of 17 units.	

Activity	Time	Description/Prompt	Materials
Explore	20+ min	Partners choose another perimeter they believe will require fractional side lengths and investigate the rectangles they can make with that perimeter. Students record all the rectangles they make. If they discover that the perimeter can be made with whole-number side lengths, they record this and save it as a counterexample.	• Grid or dot paper (see appendix), for each partnership • Square tiles
Discuss	15 min	Student share the perimeters that they investigated, including both those that required fractional side lengths and those that did not. Using these examples, the class discusses any patterns they notice and whether it is possible to find all the rectangles with a given perimeter.	Chart and markers

To the Teacher

This activity is going to push on creative thinking and mistakes. Anticipate that students will struggle to apply fraction ideas to perimeter after so much focus on whole-number side lengths in previous work with perimeter. This investigation will encourage students to think about how to decompose whole numbers into fractional parts and to begin to think about the infinite ways possible to do so. In providing an opportunity for students to think about fractions as lengths, this investigation begins to broach fractions as positions on a number line, which reinforces the infinite ways of decomposing numbers.

Encourage students to think about the perimeter as a single string of 17 units and to consider all the ways they might wrap that around a rectangle. You might ask students to think about the different ways the vertices can bend that string into four side lengths without changing its total length. Students may still struggle to think about how to decompose the perimeter into anything but whole-number side lengths. Resist the urge to tell students that they need to use fractions. Instead, ask questions that focus their attention on why it is hard to find side lengths and let students arrive at ideas for decomposing the length into partial units.

Activity

Launch

Launch the investigation by asking students, What rectangles can you make with a perimeter of 12 units? Give students a moment to turn and talk to a partner, then collect ideas by asking students to come up to grid paper (see appendix) on the document camera or a chart and draw the solutions. Be sure to encourage students to label the side lengths and provide evidence that their rectangle has a perimeter of 12 units. Students are likely to find 1×5, 2×4, and 3×3 rectangles as examples.

Tell students that today you have a challenge for them. Ask them to find as many rectangles as possible with a perimeter of 17 units. Students might say that it is impossible. If that happens, ask why, and engage the class in puzzling about what makes it possible or impossible. If your class is inclined to declare that this simply won't work, you can tell them that it is possible, and you are challenging them to figure out how.

Explore

Partners investigate the question, What different rectangles can you make with a perimeter of 17 units? Make available square tiles and grid and dot paper (see appendix). Students record all of the rectangles they make, and label the side lengths with some proof that the perimeter is 17 units. Encourage students to record the rectangles that don't work, because this might help them as they search for solutions. If students become frustrated, help them articulate why their strategies don't seem to be working. You might ask, Why is this so hard? Support students in questioning the need for whole numbers. You might ask, If whole-number sides don't work, is there something else you could try?

Discuss

Gather students together to discuss the following questions:

- What rectangles did you find? (Invite students to share their solutions and their evidence that the perimeter is 17 units. Draw attention to creative solutions, particularly those that use four fractional side lengths or side lengths with fractions other than $\frac{1}{2}$.)
- What made finding these rectangles challenging?
- Do you think we found all the possible rectangles? Why or why not?
- If we wanted to find them all, what could we do?

In this discussion, pay specific attention to how students decomposed 17 units in the two pairs of side lengths and why this perimeter required fractional side lengths. It may have been challenging for students to generate solutions that were not whole numbers, or to think about how to decompose whole numbers into fractions. Be sure to push students to explain any solutions they found, how they arrived at the rectangle's side lengths, and how they know that the perimeter is 17 units.

Explore

Ask partners to choose another perimeter that they believe will require fractional side lengths. Students investigate the perimeter they chose to prove that all the rectangles with that perimeter have some fractional side lengths. Students should record their evidence on grid or dot paper (see appendix) for others to see. If they find that the perimeter they chose does not require fractional side lengths, they should save that evidence as a counterexample and then choose a new perimeter to explore.

Discuss

Ask students to bring all their evidence to the group discussion and share the different perimeters they were able to prove require fractional side lengths, along with any counterexamples. Make a list or table to track the class's findings. This might include columns or sections for Perimeters That Must Have Fractional Sides and Perimeters That Can Have Whole-Number Sides.

Discuss the following questions:

- What patterns do you notice in the perimeters that require fractional side lengths?
- What other patterns do you see?
- Can we find all the rectangles for a given perimeter? Why or why not?

Just as in the first discussion, draw attention to any creative ways students found to make rectangles, especially rectangles with four fractional side lengths and side lengths with fractions other than $\frac{1}{2}$.

Look-Fors

- **How are students making sense of decomposing the perimeter into side lengths?** Students may struggle to think about the side lengths being fractions. In this investigation, we are intentionally leaving space for the students to figure out that fractional side lengths are needed. The frustration they may experience trying to make whole numbers work can support students in thinking creatively. You might point out the different rectangles they have tried and ask, Why didn't these work? What could you do to solve that problem? If students are really stuck, you might invite them to walk around the classroom for a moment and look at what others are trying. It is not crucial that every group figures out in the first exploration that fractional side lengths are needed. The following discussion can provide an opportunity for everyone to learn from the ideas the class creates collectively.

- **How are students justifying the perimeter of their rectangles?** To justify the perimeter, students need to recompose the side lengths into 17 units. This involves addition of whole numbers and the composing of whole numbers from fractional parts. Although this is the inverse of the decomposing work students have already done, it does require thinking in a new way about putting fractions together to make a whole. This skill of doing and undoing is an important one that threads throughout mathematics. Ask students to explain how they know that 17 units is the perimeter and to do so in a way that uses the language of making wholes.

- **How are students building on one rectangle to find another?** Once students have arrived at a solution that involves fractional side lengths, they can make small changes to the side lengths again and again to generate new solutions without starting from scratch. Ask students, How could you use this rectangle to find a new rectangle? What could you change about this rectangle to make a new one with the same perimeter? How could you be sure to keep the perimeter the same? These kinds of questions can support students in thinking systematically and making connections between addition, equivalence, and fractions.

Reflect

How are fractions connected to length?

BIG IDEA 8

Being Flexible with Numbers

In the introduction to Big Idea 3 we talked about the research of Gray and Tall which showed that the most successful students are those who are flexible with numbers. Many curriculum standards and district mandates cite fluency as an important goal, which causes parents and teachers to focus on number drills and memorization. The reduction of mathematics to a set of math facts to be memorized is one of the reasons we have a nation of mathematically traumatized students. Fluency has nothing to do with speed; students who are fluent with numbers are those who are comfortable with numbers, which rarely comes about when mathematics is associated with speed. Instead of encouraging students to blindly memorize, ask them to think visually and creatively about numbers so that they develop number sense and think conceptually about numbers. It can be helpful to commit math facts to memory, but not through blind memorization and not through focusing on speed, which has its own set of problems. We discuss the damage caused by blind memorization and by speed-based practices, and offer a set of engaging ways to teach math facts in our paper "Fluency without Fear," which can be accessed on youcubed.org. If you give students plenty of opportunities to work with numbers and with math facts, conceptually and visually, they will start to remember them—with meaning—and be able to use them.

In our Visualize activity, we provide a lesson based on the structure of number talks. The lesson starts by asking students how many they see, using square tiles, so that students again see the connection between area and the operation of multiplication, as in Big Idea 4, Tiling to Understand Area. After students have worked together as a class, they will work in small groups conducting their own mini number talks with each other. This is another opportunity to encourage and value different ways of seeing and send the powerful message that mathematics is about diversity of ideas and perspectives.

In our Play activity, we invite students to play How Close to 100? This is an activity that we included in "Fluency without Fear" and that has been extremely popular with both teachers and students since its release. Some teachers have told us about successful parent evenings where they have invited entire halls of parents to play How Close to 100? together, to help parents learn about the value of approaching math facts conceptually and visually, rather than through the use of flash cards or other damaging activities. In this activity, students work in pairs with the goal of being the first to finish their own 10×10 grid. At each roll of the dice, students multiply the two numbers together and draw a visual array of the solution with the goal of completing their grid, which means they need to be strategic in their placement of the rectangles they draw. Students really enjoy this game at the same time as they are learning math facts numerically, visually, and deeply.

In our Investigate activity, students are asked to look at a growing pattern of squares. Growing patterns are a good way to encourage number flexibility, as students will see the pattern's growth in different ways. We encourage you to take time to hear from as many students as possible when discussing the first pattern in the launch of this investigation. Students will see the pattern differently, and each way they see it is a different number representation. Students may be astonished to see that each of the different number representations results in the same number, the area of the rectangle. Analyzing the different visual representations, number sentences, and connections between them builds the foundation for number flexibility. The final connection we offer comes through asking students to find the areas of their rectangles on a multiplication table. We encourage students to see and come to know the multiplication table as a table of interesting patterns—not a list of facts to memorize. Seeing the growing patterns as data points plotted on the multiplication table will support students in seeing unique visual patterns and making connections across the operation of multiplication.

Jo Boaler

How Many Do You See?

Snapshot

Students build flexibility with multiplicative thinking by creating arrays and developing creative ways of seeing how many the array represents.

> Connection to CCSS
> 3.OA.3, 3.OA.1, 3.OA.7
> 3.MD.7

Agenda

Activity	Time	Description/Prompt	Materials
Launch	10 min	Make or draw a 5 × 6 array. Show the array to students briefly and ask, How many do you see? How do you see it? Collect students' different ways of seeing the quantity, and celebrate creative strategies.	• Optional: 30 square tiles • Chart and markers
Explore	20–30 min	In groups of four, students take turns creating their own arrays and asking the rest of the group for the ways they see the quantity.	Square tiles and file folder, for each group
Discuss	15 min	Discuss the different strategies that students developed and the creative ways they saw quantity. Introduce an array with some squares missing (or added) and ask students how many they see and how. Name these as arrays-more-or-less.	Chart and markers
Explore	20+ min	In groups of four, students take turns creating their own arrays-more-or-less and asking the rest of the group for the ways they see the quantity.	Square tiles and file folder, for each group

(Continued)

Activity	Time	Description/Prompt	Materials
Discuss	10 min	Discuss the different strategies that students developed and how these were related to the strategies they used for complete arrays. Celebrate surprising, creative, and elegant strategies.	Chart and markers

To the Teacher

This lesson is a variation on dot talks (Parrish, 2010), in which we show students a collection of dots arranged to support decomposing and subitizing to count and ask, How many do you see? How do you see it? In dot talks done with young children, the goal is to support counting of small groups of objects, typically 12 or fewer. But with older students, dot talks can support students in thinking about how patterns help counting of far larger collections by arranging the dots or squares in arrays. In this lesson, we aim to build flexibility with numbers built on counting, skip counting, addition, and multiplication. The images students create provide an opportunity to decompose the array's area into smaller, more manageable pieces, and then recompose the pieces to find the total. Because of the visual connection to arrays, number flexibility is also related to area and the idea that both number and space can be decomposed and recomposed without changing how much it represents.

If your students have not yet had experience with dot talks in particular, or number talks more generally, you will want to spend some time in the launch explicitly describing the expectations and the routine. Students will need to know that they should give a private signal, such as a thumbs-up, when they have an answer, to allow others time to think. Students will also need to understand that the focus of these talks is on how they see the quantity and what their process was. This requires becoming aware of what they are thinking as it happens, and such metacognition is challenging work that requires practice. This is a great place to give lots of practice and to provide support for students to start to watch their own thinking.

Activity

Launch

Launch the activity by showing students a 5 × 6 array of square tiles on the document camera or a 5 × 6 array of dots drawn on a chart. Ask the class, How many do you see? Show the image for a few seconds, and then cover it. The goal is for students to figure out how many, without counting by ones.

Take some ideas from students of how many squares they saw, then press students to explain by asking, How did you see it? Record the different ways students saw how many squares (or dots) there were. For instance, students may have broken the shape into two rectangles of 5 × 3 and then added them together or doubled. Another student might see a 5 × 5 square and then one more row of 5. Celebrate the variations and creativity in the ways students saw the quantity.

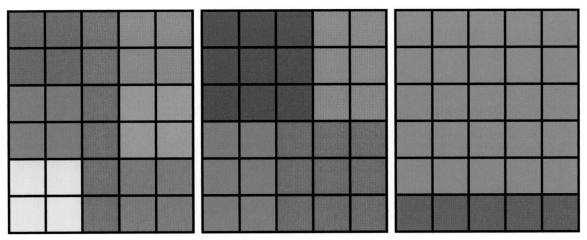

A few ways students may see the 5 x 6 arrangement

Describe the activity that students will be doing in small groups today.

Explore

In groups of four, students take turns creating arrays and figuring out how many they see. Each group will need a collection of square tiles or chips and a file folder for covering the array.

Taking turns around the group, one student will make an array using the tiles behind a file folder so others cannot see until it is ready. Then the student will show the other group members the array and ask, How many do you see? Just as with the whole class, they show the array to the group briefly and then re-cover it.

Each member of the group then tells how many they saw and describes how they saw it. The goal is to arrive at creative and efficient ways to see how many.

Discuss

Discuss as a class the following questions:

- What strategies did you develop for seeing how many?
- What creative or interesting ways did you hear from others in your group?
- What made seeing how many challenging?
- Were there some arrays that were harder than others? Why?

As students discuss their strategies, record examples of what the class has developed on chart paper for others to reference.

Introduce the next part of the activity by making the array shown in the figure here with square tiles on the document camera and showing it to the class. Ask them, How many do you see? How do you see it?

Give students a moment to think, cover the image, and take answers. Focus on the different ways students see how many. Students might decompose the shape into two or more rectangles and add them together, or see it as a 4×4 square with two missing tiles. Students could also see this shape as a 4×3 rectangle with two extra squares added on. Tell students we are going to call these shapes *arrays-more-or-less.*

Explore

Students play the same game, but this time making arrays-more-or-less instead of complete arrays. Encourage students to come up with creative ways of seeing how many and to think about which ways seem to be most efficient.

Discuss

Discuss as a class the following questions:

- What strategies did you develop?
- How were your strategies the same as those for complete arrays? What was different?
- What were the most efficient or elegant strategies?
- What were the most creative strategies you heard?
- What is a strategy that you heard someone in your group use that surprised you?

Add new strategies to your chart of strategies for arrays, showing any ways that these are connected.

Look-Fors

- **Are students trying to count by 1s?** Students may be tempted to count each tile to find the total, believing that this will lead to the most accurate answer or because it is the most comfortable strategy for them. Encourage students to think about these questions: How many of the tiles do you really need to count to know how many there are? Which tiles do you need to count to figure out how many? For instance, once students know that a row contains 6 tiles, they can infer that the row beneath it also has 6 tiles. How can they use that pattern to help them figure out how many? It is not necessary that students use multiplication or rely on remembered facts. Students will build fluency by seeing and using patterns flexibly, and this activity can be a good place to start.

- **Are students making reasonable-sized arrays and offering reasonable time for their groups to look?** It takes some learning to create arrays, or arrays-more-or-less, that are an appropriate size for this activity, and to provide just enough time for others to see well, without counting by 1s. You may want to provide some guidance to students or to ask them to generate some guidelines for both of these choices. The other factor to consider is how much time it takes to construct the arrays. Very large arrays, such as a 10×9, would be both difficult to see and time consuming to construct. Encourage students to use the feedback of their groups to select arrays that are an interesting challenge. If a student hears their group members calling for more time, it is probably needed. If answers are all automatic, the array may have been too small or simple. Support students in attending to feedback and making adjustments.

- **Are students trying different strategies as they play?** The goal of this big idea is to build flexibility with numbers, which can only be done if students try different strategies, look for new ways of seeing, and make decisions about which strategies make the most sense depending on the circumstances. As you watch students play, look for and celebrate moments when students think flexibly, invent a new way, or adopt a strategy shared by another student. If you notice any students getting stuck using the same strategy regardless of the numbers or image, you might slow them down and ask if there is another way they could see it. You can encourage them to try it a new way on the next image. It can be useful to specifically name how this kind of flexibility helps grow their brain.

Reflect

What do you think are the most useful ways to see how many are in an array?

Reference

Parrish, S. (2010). *Number talks: Whole number computation.* Sausalito, CA: Math Solutions.

How Close to 100?

Snapshot

Students build flexibility with multiplication through the area game How Close to 100?

Connection to CCSS
3.OA.7, 3.OA.3, 3.OA.1
3.MD.5, 3.MD.6, 3.MD.7

Agenda

Activity	Time	Description/Prompt	Materials
Launch	10–15 min	Show students how to play How Close to 100? and describe how the game ends.	• How Close to 100? recording sheet, to display • 2 dice • Colors
Play	30+ min	Partners play How Close to 100? and develop strategies for getting closer to 100 by playing the game repeatedly.	• How Close to 100? recording sheet, multiple copies per partnership • Dice, two per partnership • Colors
Discuss	10–15 min	Discuss the strategies students have developed and what makes a good move. Discuss what makes it hard to cover the board completely.	
Extend	30+ min	Students play a variation of the game in which they can place on the board any rectangle that has the same area as the rectangle they have rolled on the dice.	• How Close to 100? recording sheet, multiple copies per partnership • Dice, two per partnership • Colors

To the Teacher

This game first appeared on youcubed.org in 2014, and it found an instant home in classrooms across the world. Students love playing the game, which creates countless opportunities to think flexibly about number. The game itself is flexible, leaving room for you and your students to create variations that make the game more challenging as students build flexibility in the original game. We have seen teachers change the size and shape of the game board, making it larger or nonrectangular. We have seen variations with three dice, in which students choose two dice to add together to become a side length. We've provided another variation in the extension to this activity, in which students can place any rectangle with an area equivalent to that of the product of the dice rolled. We encourage you to experiment with your own variations that excite your students and build flexibility through play.

Activity

Launch

Launch the lesson by showing students the How Close to 100? recording sheet on a document camera. Play the game as a class for a few rounds simply to show the rules. Don't give away any strategies about where to place rectangles; just make sure students understand how to play. Tell students that at the end of the game, when they can no longer place a

A student completing their game board

rectangle on the board, they will count up the area covered to find out how close to 100 they got. In the next round they play, students should try to get even closer to 100 and think about how they could do that.

Play

Students play How Close to 100? in partners. Each partnership will need a How Close to 100? recording sheet and two dice. It is helpful for each player to have a different color pencil or marker. Note that students can play alone if they would like to.

Game Directions

- Players take turns. On a turn, roll two dice. The numbers on the dice represent the length and width of a rectangle. Record the array made by these number anywhere on the grid you want.
- Then record the multiplication number sentence with the rectangle's area in the recording space under the grid.
- The goal is to cover the entire game board with arrays. Play continues until either
  - The grid is perfectly covered. Hooray!
  - A player rolls two numbers and both partners agree that the array cannot be placed anywhere on the grid. Count up the area covered. How close to 100 did you get? Play again and try to get closer.

Encourage partners to play a few rounds to develop strategies for getting closer to 100.

Discuss

Discuss the following questions:

- How did you figure out how close to 100 you got?
- What are some strategies that you developed for playing the game?
- How did you decide where to place your rectangles?
- What makes a good move?
- What made it hard to get to 100?

We encourage you to find time for students to play this game again after this discussion so that they can try the ideas that surfaced and get more opportunities to build flexibility.

Extend

The game can be adapted for greater challenge and flexibility. In this variation, when a player rolls the dice and gets the dimensions, they can place on the grid any rectangle that has an equivalent area. For instance, if a player rolls 2 and 6, the area of that rectangle is 12. The player can determine that area and then place any area 12 rectangle that will fit on the grid, such as a 3×4 (though not a 1×12, because it will not fit on our game board). This variation encourages students to think about the different ways to make rectangles with the same area, building flexibility with factor pairs.

Look-Fors

- **How are students placing their rectangles on the board?** Students can place their rectangles anywhere, but some ways of packing rectangles in are more efficient and can enable the group to get closer to 100. If you see students placing the rectangles randomly, leaving narrow gaps, or positioning them as islands, ask questions about how they are making their decisions. It can be productive to let students play the game all the way through and then reflect on what happened after the game is over. You might ask, What would have made it easier to cover the board and get close to 100? What made it hard when you got to the end of the game? What could you try differently in the next round?

- **How are students finding the area of a rectangle?** Notice the ways they are figuring out each rectangle's area. You may notice some counting, skip counting, or the use of fingers. For some rectangles, students may simply know the product of the two numbers, particularly when one of the factors is 1 or 2. Even when students know these facts, ask them *how* they know. It is powerful for students to develop visual explanations for these patterns. For instance, students might know that any number multiplied by 1 is itself, but it is more robust understanding to be able to explain that we can see it in the one row of squares in the rectangle. Ask students to explain the patterns they are noticing and using so that they can apply them to many situations.

- **How are students figuring out how much of the board is covered?** There are several ways to figure this out. Students might find the sum of the products at the bottom of the recording sheet, or count all the squares covered on the board. Alternatively, students might count the uncovered squares and subtract this from 100. This is a great example of the way need can create efficiency. As students play this game they will likely arrive at increasingly efficient strategies for seeing if they have gotten closer to 100 this time around. In the discussion, invite students to share these different ways and use it as an opportunity to talk about efficiency so that students have language for naming this quality of a strategy.

Reflect

What advice would you offer someone learning to play How Close to 100? What makes a good move?

How Close to 100?

1. _____ x _____ = _____

2. _____ x _____ = _____

3. _____ x _____ = _____

4. _____ x _____ = _____

5. _____ x _____ = _____

6. _____ x _____ = _____

7. _____ x _____ = _____

8. _____ x _____ = _____

9. _____ x _____ = _____

10. _____ x _____ = _____

Tile and Table Patterns

Snapshot

Students create growing patterns with rectangles and then locate those rectangles on the multiplication table and see what new patterns this reveals.

> Connection to CCSS
> 3.OA.9
> 3.OA.1, 3.OA.3, 3.OA.7
> 3.MD.7

Agenda

Activity	Time	Description/Prompt	Materials
Launch	10–15 min	Show students the tower pattern and ask what patterns they see. Discuss how the pattern grows. Then ask them to locate these rectangles on the multiplication table. Discuss what patterns they see now, and predict where the next rectangle in the pattern will be in the table.	• Tower Pattern sheet, to display • Multiplication Table sheet, to display
Explore	30–40+ min	Partners create their own growing rectangle patterns on grid or dot paper and then locate their rectangles on the multiplication table, extending the pattern as far as it goes on the table. Partners try this with different patterns, color-coding them on the multiplication table and making observations.	• Grid or dot paper (see appendix), multiple sheets per partnership • Square tiles • Multiplication Table sheet, at least one per partnership • Colors
Discuss	20 min	Partners present the most interesting pattern they created, along with where it is located on the multiplication table. Discuss the patterns student see in the multiplication table, and generate questions that students are wondering about now.	• Multiplication Table sheet, to display • Colors

To the Teacher

This investigation involves creating, decomposing, and then recomposing patterns in different forms. Students first need a solid experience during the launch of what a visual growing pattern of rectangles can look like, so that they can create their own. In the tower pattern, we have created a sequence of rectangles in which each side gets longer by 1 unit to make the next member of the pattern. Our pattern starts with a 2 × 1 rectangle. This same pattern would result in different rectangles if started with a 1 × 1 or a 3 × 1 rectangle. Other rectangle patterns might add a unit (or more) to only one side, such as the sequence 2 × 1, 2 × 2, 2 × 3, . . . This sequence creates a growing tower with a base that is unchanged. Once students get started, they will find lots of ways to make rectangle patterns grow. Often students do this visually first, rather than numerically. Encourage any ways students come up with to represent growth; all add depth and flexibility to students' understanding of multiplicative patterns.

When these rectangular patterns are plotted on the multiplication table, new patterns emerge that can enable students to predict and extend the sequence they have started visually. Students can also compare the different kinds of patterns created based on how they appear on the table. For instance, there are patterns that appear as diagonals, whereas others may be clear vertical or horizontal stripes, and some may hop and skip across the table. Be sure to allow time to talk about why some patterns appear similar on the multiplication table and reason about this similarity.

One other note about the multiplication table. We often think of it as just that, a table, when in fact it is an array. The product of 3 × 2 is in a square that forms the vertex of a 3 × 2 rectangle. As students are looking for their rectangles on the multiplication table, take advantage of any observations students make that connect the table itself to arrays and the rectangles they are looking for. You might even challenge students to draw their rectangles right on the table to see what they find. This is a useful way of thinking about this tool that is rarely explored, and we encourage you to look for opportunities to make the connection between the table and area. We have also started the multiplication table in with 1 × 1 in the lower left corner. We have done this because students may see the patterns growing upward and outward. As they identify the products of the lengths and widths of their rectangles, they will be doing some early plotting of points on a coordinate grid. This is another visual connection that we want to help students make.

10	10	20	30	40	50	60	70	80	90	100
9	9	18	27	36	45	54	63	72	81	90
8	8	16	24	32	40	48	56	64	72	80
7	7	14	21	28	35	42	49	56	63	70
6	6	12	18	24	30	36	42	48	54	60
5	5	10	15	20	25	30	35	40	45	50
4	4	8	12	16	20	24	28	32	36	40
3	3	6	9	12	15	18	21	24	27	30
2	2	4	6	8	10	12	14	16	18	20
1	1	2	3	4	5	6	7	8	9	10
x	1	2	3	4	5	6	7	8	9	10

A 2 x 3 rectangle is shown with a point representing the area at the number 6. A 5 x 6 rectangle is shown to have an area of 30.

Activity

Launch

Launch the investigation by showing students the Tower Pattern image on the document camera. Ask students, What patterns do you see? Take students' ideas for different ways to describe the rectangles and how they grow. Be sure to draw attention to ideas that include the dimensions and the areas.

Mindset Mathematics, Grade 3

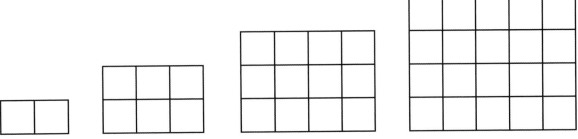

Tower pattern showing horizontal and vertical growth

Show the multiplication table and ask students to study it for a while. After they have become aware of the change in orientation of the table, ask, Where are these rectangles on the table? How do you know? Be sure to get students to justify where the dimensions are and where the area is. Color in the squares that represent each rectangle, wherever students found them. They may have seen them horizontally or vertically. Either is fine.

10	10	20	30	40	50	60	70	80	90	100
9	9	18	27	36	45	54	63	72	81	90
8	8	16	24	32	40	48	56	64	72	80
7	7	14	21	28	35	42	49	56	63	70
6	6	12	18	24	30	36	42	48	54	60
5	5	10	15	20	25	30	35	40	45	50
4	4	8	12	16	20	24	28	32	36	40
3	3	6	9	12	15	18	21	24	27	30
2	2	4	6	8	10	12	14	16	18	20
1	1	2	3	4	5	6	7	8	9	10
x	1	2	3	4	5	6	7	8	9	10

The tower pattern rectangles shown on the multiplication table

Big Idea 8: Being Flexible with Numbers

Ask, What patterns do you notice? Take some ideas. Ask, What might be next? Where would we find it on the table? How do you know?

Explore

Partners create rectangle patterns that grow, like the one the class examined together. These patterns can extend as far as partners like and be simple or complex, depending on students' interest. Make square tiles available for students who want to build the rectangles physically. Students then record their patterns on grid or dot paper (see appendix).

Partners then look for where this pattern shows up on the multiplication table. They color-code this pattern as far as it can extend on the multiplication table. Partners discuss the question, What do you notice?

Students create, record, and color-code as many patterns as they can to investigate the patterns on the multiplication table. Be sure students use different colors for different patterns so that they can distinguish them on the table. If their tables get too crowded, you may want to offer them a fresh copy.

Discuss

Ask partners to choose the most interesting patterns they created and present them to the class. Students show both their drawings and how the pattern shows up on the multiplication table. Ask students to share what it was they found interesting about the pattern they constructed. As partners present, create a shared class color-coded multiplication table with the patterns the class found.

Discuss as a class the following questions:

- What patterns did we discover?
- What do you notice about the kinds of patterns we found?
- What patterns appear to be similar on the multiplication table? Why do you think that is?
- What patterns surprised you?
- What do you wonder now?

If students develop interesting questions about rectangle patterns and the multiplication table, we encourage you to explore these questions with students.

Look-Fors

- **Are students' rectangle patterns growing consistently?** This is the first challenge in this investigation: to create a consistent pattern that grows in the same way from one member of the sequence to the next. Ask students to describe how they were changing the first rectangle to get the next one. Push them to be precise and clear. This does not mean that they need to speak formally, but rather that they use language that can be transferred to the next rectangle and repeated. For instance, students might say that they added a layer or row to the right edge. Then the next question is, Is that what you did to each rectangle to get the next? Support students in thinking carefully about their sequence before they move on to the multiplication table. If students do make mistakes, however, the multiplication table will help them see where and how the pattern changed track.

- **How are students connecting rectangle side lengths, area, and multiplication?** When students move from drawing rectangles to locating them on the multiplication table, they will need to consider how to describe these rectangles numerically. This involves the lengths of the sides and the area. It is worth asking students to explain why a multiplication table can show the patterns in the rectangles. Why not an addition table? How are rectangles, area, and multiplication connected? How can we see that connection on the multiplication table?

- **Are students trying different kinds of patterns?** Once students get started making growing rectangle patterns, you might notice that they are making the same kinds of patterns again and again. For instance, students might start with a tower 3 squares wide and add a layer to the top, creating a 3×1, 3×2, $3 \times 3, \ldots$ pattern. They might then do this again starting with a tower 4 squares wide and then starting with a tower 2 squares wide. If you notice this repetition, you might ask why the students are exploring this same kind of pattern over and over. Students may have a compelling reason. For instance, they may be wondering if the pattern will always lead to a column or row on the multiplication table. This would be a great question for students to spend time exploring. However, if students are simply stuck in a rut, help them brainstorm other ways to generate patterns so that they can see some contrast with the patterns they have already tried.

- **Are students connecting area to the multiplication table?** As described in To the Teacher, it can be a powerful connection for students to see the rectangles they are making represented directly on the multiplication table to help this tool make sense. Look for opportunities to connect the rectangles to the table, such as when students run their fingers across rows and columns. You might point out where they have touched the table and how it connects back to their drawing. If students are having trouble finding their rectangles on the table, you might prompt them to draw the rectangle directly on the table, starting at the top left. In the launch discussion, lean on the questions, Where are these rectangles on the table? How do you know? You might ask if anyone can prove it visually using the table. Even if only one or two students notice this connection, it will be an important discovery they can share with the whole class, which could help everyone think about the connection between area and multiplication.

Reflect

What pattern most surprised you? Why?

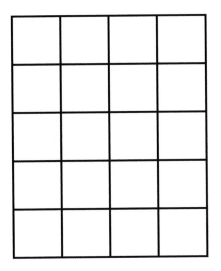

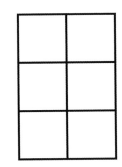

Multiplication Table

x	1	2	3	4	5	6	7	8	9	10
10	10	20	30	40	50	60	70	80	90	100
9	9	18	27	36	45	54	63	72	81	90
8	8	16	24	32	40	48	56	64	72	80
7	7	14	21	28	35	42	49	56	63	70
6	6	12	18	24	30	36	42	48	54	60
5	5	10	15	20	25	30	35	40	45	50
4	4	8	12	16	20	24	28	32	36	40
3	3	6	9	12	15	18	21	24	27	30
2	2	4	6	8	10	12	14	16	18	20
1	1	2	3	4	5	6	7	8	9	10

Appendix

$\frac{1}{4}$ " Grid Paper

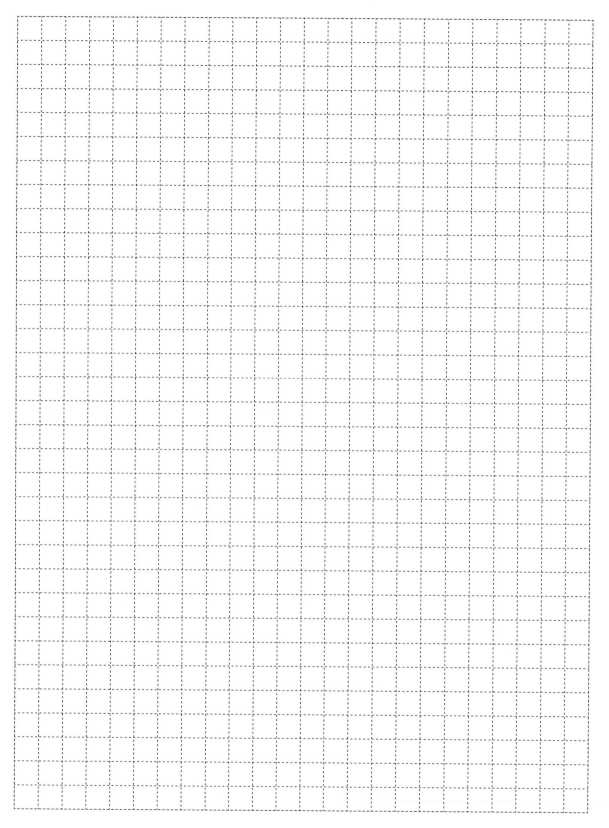

 **Grid Paper**

1″ Grid Paper

$\frac{1}{4}''$ Dot Paper

Centimeter Dot Paper

Appendix

Isometric Dot Paper

Hundred Grids

About the Authors

 **Dr. Jo Boaler** is a professor of mathematics education at Stanford University, and the cofounder of Youcubed. She is the author of the first MOOC on mathematics teaching and learning. Former roles have included being the Marie Curie Professor of Mathematics Education in England, a mathematics teacher in London comprehensive schools, and a lecturer and researcher at King's College, London. Her work has been published in the *Times,* the *Telegraph,* the *Wall Street Journal,* and many other news outlets. The BBC recently named Jo one of the eight educators "changing the face of education."

 **Jen Munson** is a postdoctoral fellow at Northwestern University, a professional developer, and a former classroom teacher. She earned her PhD in mathematics education from Stanford University. Her research focuses on how coaching can support teachers in growing their mathematics instructional practices, particularly in the elementary grades, and how teacher-student interactions influence equitable math learning. Before leaving the classroom to coach, she taught elementary and middle school in Washington, DC, Chicago, and the Seattle area.

Cathy Williams is the cofounder and director of Youcubed. She completed an applied mathematics major at University of California, San Diego before becoming a high school math teacher for 18 years in San Diego County. After teaching, she became a county office coordinator and then district mathematics director. As part of her leadership work, Cathy has designed professional development and curriculum. Her district work in the Vista Unified School District won a California Golden Bell for instruction in 2013 for the K–12 Innovation Cohort in mathematics. In Vista, Cathy worked with Jo changing the way mathematics was taught across the district.

Acknowledgments

We thank Jill Marsal, our book agent. We are also very grateful to our Youcubed army of teachers. Thanks to Robin Anderson for drawing the network diagram on our cover. Finally, we thank our children—and dogs!—for putting up with our absences from family life as we worked to bring our vision of mathematical mindset tasks to life.

Index

Cordero, Montse, 1

Counting: movement in relation to, 52; perimeter, 59–60, 61, 63; skip-counting, 86, 88–89; squares, 130–131

Cover Up Close-Up sheet, 191–192, 193–194, 198

Cover Up game activity: agenda for, 191–192; comprehension questions for, 197–198; Cover Up Close-Up sheet for, 191–192, 193–194, 198; Cover Up Game Boards sheet for, 191–192, 195, 199; dice for, 191–192, 194–195; discussion on, 195–196; exploration in, 196; extension of, 196–197; for fractions, 184, 191–201; game directions for, 195; I Spy $\frac{1}{2}$ activity in relation to, 192–193; launch of, 193–194; teacher notes for, 192; Unit Fraction Sort sheets for, 192, 196, 200–201

Cover Up Game Boards sheet, 191–192, 195, 199

Cracker sharing activity: agenda for, 78–79; comprehension questions for, 81–83; discussion on, 80, 81; exploration in, 80–81; extension of, 81; fractions in relation to, 76, 82–83; launch of, 80; for multiplication and division, 75–76, 78–84; Sharing Crackers Organizer sheet for, 78, 80, 81, 84; teacher notes for, 79

Creativity: How Many Do You See? game for, 211–216; with I Spy $\frac{1}{2}$ activity, 154, 155; with investigation activities, 14; with journals, 5–6; memorization in relation to, 209; mistakes in relation to, 184, 203; with perimeter finding, 52, 69; with play activities, 13; for problem-solving, 8; with visual activities, 12

Cuisenaire rods: as classroom manipulatives, 125–126; patterns with, 127, 130; for

perimeter of rectangles, 125–126, 127–131

Curriculum standards: Common Core, 9; fluency in relation to, 209

D

Data: accuracy of, 39, 47; patterns in, 52; relevance, 23–24

Data collection planning: brainstorm for, 45–46; car color activity for, 24, 41–49

Data interpretation: animal graph activity for, 23, 25–35; Inspector Graph-It for, 23–24, 36–40

Data tables: for animal height, 36, 37, 40; for animal tongue lengths, 26, 29–30, 35

Detection of errors, 23–24, 36–40

Dice: as classroom manipulative, 86; for Cover Up game activity, 191–192, 194–195; for How Close to 100? game, 210, 217–221. *See also* Dozens of dice activity

Discussion: alphabet activity for area, 114; on animal graph activity, 29, 30; on area sharing activity, 122, 123; on area/perimeter connection activity, 145–146; on car color activity, 44–45; on Cover Up game activity, 195–196; on cracker sharing activity, 80, 81; on dozens of dice activity, 88; on fractional walk activity, 205–206; on geoboards activity for area, 104; geoboards activity for perimeter, 68–69; on How Close to 100? game, 219; on How Many Do You See? game, 214–215; on I Spy $\frac{1}{2}$ activity, 155; on Inspector Graph-It, 38; on paper folding activity, 19–21; on parts as whole activity, 188; on playing with pairs activity, 94, 95; posters for group work, 17–18; on rods around activity, 130; on shapes of $\frac{1}{2}$ activity, 174–175; on spotting $\frac{1}{2}$ activity, 162–163;

on squares/near-squares activity, 136–137; on string activity for perimeter, 55–56; on 36-unit walk, 61–62; on tower pattern activity, 226

Distance, 202–207

Division: multiplication in relation to, 75–76, 78–84; reflection on, 83

Dot talks, 212

Dozens of dice activity: agenda for, 85; color coding for, 76; comprehension questions for, 88–89; discussion on, 88; Dozens of Dice image sheet for, 85, 86, 88, 90; extension of, 88; launch of, 86–87; for multiplication and repeated addition, 85–90; teacher notes for, 86

Dozens of Dice image sheet, 85, 86, 88, 90

Drawings: for fractional walk activity, 204; for How Many Do You See? game, 211, 213; for parts as whole activity, 187, 188; for rods around activity, 128, 129; for shapes of $\frac{1}{2}$ activity, 173–174; for squares/near-squares activity, 136–137; for string activity for perimeter, 55, 56; for tower pattern activity, 223–224, 225, 226

Driscoll, Mark, 8

E

8 × 8 Boards sheets, 171, 173–174, 177

Einstein, Albert, 13

Embodied cognition, 51, 54

Encouragement: for fractions, 203; for game design, 196–197; for group work, 17–18; for student reasoning, 7–8

Enjoyment: play activities for, 13; of skepticism, 8

Equal groups: cracker sharing activity for, 75–76, 78–84; dozens of dice activity for, 76, 85–90; playing with pairs activity for, 76–77, 91–97